the *Spirit* of Christmas

the *Spirit* of Christmas

Tommy Barnett, John Bevere,
Creflo A. Dollar Jr., John Hagee,
Jackie McCullough, James Robison,
and Ron M. Phillips

THOMAS NELSON PUBLISHERS
Nashville

Published in Nashville, Tennessee, by Thomas Nelson, Inc.

Library of Congress Cataloging-in-Publication Data

p.   cm.

ISBN 0-7852-6949-5

1. Christmas Meditations.   I. Barnett, Tommy.

BV45.S65   1999

242' . 335—dc21   99-15322

CIP

Printed in the United States of America.

1 2 3 4 5 6 – 04 03 02 01 00 99

Interior Photo Credits:

Photodisc, Tony Stone Images, Image Bank, Photonica (Cosmo & Action and Miyoko Komine)

Contents

Introduction ❧

Christmas

is not just a story of

angels, shepherds, Mary, Joseph,

and the baby Jesus.

The heavenly host who appeared to the shepherds at Christ's birth announced peace on earth, declaring the inaugural step for reconciliation between a righteous God and sinful man. The peace declared by the angels is twofold— positional and experiential. When we trust Christ for salvation, we receive positional peace from God. We are forgiven and released from the penalty of sin, justified, and restored to positional relationship and fellowship with the God of the universe. ❧ The experiential peace of God empowers us to face life's battles, problems, and uncertainties. This peace, which flows from the Spirit of God, anchors our minds and calms our anxieties. It provides companionship to the lonely, comfort to the brokenhearted, and it profoundly affects our relationships with others.

Both aspects of this divine peace—positional and experiential—were encompassed in the original Christmas message heralded by the angels: "Peace on earth!" God's gift of peace, the Prince of Peace, is the true spirit of Christmas.

The Spirit of Christmas is a distinctive collection of messages from seven of America's most beloved ministers that will draw you beyond the bright decorations, extravagant gifts, and holiday frills to experience the true meaning of this season. These people not only provide penetrating insights from God's Word, but they also open their hearts to share intimate feelings and personal experiences that truly reflect the spirit of Christmas.

"Call Him Wonderful" by Dr. Ron Phillips examines the significance of the names of Jesus Christ given in Isaiah 9:6. This prophecy, recorded seven hundred years before Jesus was born, gives the glorious fivefold name of Jesus Christ. His wonderful names shone brilliantly against the dark background of a world that had lost its way. Dr. Phillips shares how Isaiah was allowed a look through the telescope of prophecy to see a new day dawning, a new kingdom, and a new kind of King, Jesus Christ.

John Bevere draws from a personal encounter with God to address the question of our value in "Christmas Declares Our Value." In a time of changing values and situational ethics when what mankind values in one generation is resented in the next, he

calls us to consider our true value to God. He directs us to biblical passages that confirm our true worth, and he challenges us to explore the unfathomable value that God places on everyone who is called by His name.

Jackie McCullough issues a mandate for us to experience the true spirit of Christmas in a message entitled "Celebrate the Gift of Worship." In this selection, you will be transported back in time to endure the rigors of Joseph and Mary's journey to Bethlehem, learning that even in the midst of hardship, God is at work fulfilling His plan in your life. You will see how God broke into the routine of common men like the shepherds to fulfill His purposes. You will be challenged to celebrate Jesus, His advent, and the peace He brings to those whose hearts are ready to receive Him.

Tommy Barnett opens his heart to share the deeply moving story of his wife, Marja, relating her experiences in "A Star, a Stable, and the Savior." He focuses attention on the star that led the wise men, challenging us to be reflections that guide others to Jesus. He shares how our Savior was born in a smelly stable into a real family with few worldly advantages. He was a refugee to Egypt, and He understood heartache, disappointment, and rejection. He can identify with us because He has been through it. In a final challenge, we are encouraged to penetrate the darkness of this world with the message of a star, a stable, and the Savior.

James Robison shares a moving personal experience in "No Gifts That Christmas." Your heart will be touched by the memory of his shattered expectations as a nine-year-old child when he received no presents for Christmas, an experience that actually culminated in his finding peace with God. Your heart will be stirred as he draws on his intimate involvement with world missions to challenge you to receive and then share with others the One who is more than a baby wrapped in swaddling cloths. He is the gift of life itself.

Writing "The Secret of Peace and Goodwill," John Hagee conveys a powerful message that examines our world today and questions, "Where is peace on earth?" He surveys deteriorating conditions in a world ravaged by murder, drugs, rape, incest, child abuse, and corruption, and he then asks, "Where is the peace that the angels

Jesus Christ
the Prince of Peace

declared?" God's peace is not universal, but reigns only where men and women will pay the price. The price of peace in your home, your life, this nation, and our world is absolute surrender to God and His Word.

Finally, in his expressive, charismatic style in "How to Receive the Spirit of Christmas," Creflo A. Dollar Jr. shares a message that invites us to have a "Mary" Christmas. Drawing spiritual parallels from what occurred in the Virgin Mary's life, Dr. Dollar challenges us to be impregnated with the Word of God and give birth to the miraculous.

The stirring messages of these seven gifted communicators will enable you to experience the true spirit of Christmas—God's peace come to earth, clothed in human form—Jesus Christ, the Prince of Peace. 🎵

Call Him Wonderful

RON M. PHILLIPS

In Shakespeare's classic play, Juliet asked Romeo, "What's in a name? That which we call a rose by any other name would smell as sweet." In spite of the sentiment in those words, the truth is that we are people, not plants, and our names carry great significance. Someone once said, "The sweetest sound on earth is your own name spoken tenderly by a friend."

A GOOD NAME

In biblical times, a person's name directly indicated his character. If we explore the pages of a Hebrew Bible, we find that the Hebrew word for "name" is *shem*, the name also given to one of Noah's sons. This word comes from a root word meaning "to set a mark." A child was often named according to something that "marked" the child. For instance, the godly woman Hannah prayed earnestly for a child to break the curse of barrenness on her life. When God granted her prayer and a son was born, she rejoiced as she named the boy Samuel, which meant "asked of God."

Jewish parents felt that a name given to a child was significant, and the character that developed in the child's life would forever color that name. Many times a name would become synonymous with fame, renown, and heroic reputation, such as in the case of David. God Himself blessed the name of David, saying, "I have been with you wherever you have gone, and have cut off all your enemies from before you, and have made you a great name, like the name of the great men who are on the earth" (2 Sam. 7:9 NKJV).

Unfortunately, a name could also come to represent evil. After years of being under the rule of a fiendish

queen whose wickedness caused heartache in the land of the chosen people, few Jewish families consider the name Jezebel for their baby girls!

GOD'S MATCHLESS NAME

In the Old Testament revelation, God's name is of particular importance. He revealed Himself to Moses by using the Hebrew tetragram YHWH, or Yahweh (Jehovah), which issues forth the meaning "I AM WHO I AM":

> God said to Moses, "I AM WHO I AM." And He said, "Thus you shall say to the children of Israel, 'I AM has sent me to you.'" Moreover God said to Moses, "Thus you shall say to the children of Israel: 'The LORD God of your fathers, the God of Abraham, the God of Isaac, and the God of Jacob, has sent me to you. This is My name forever, and this is My memorial to all generations.'" (Ex. 3:14–15 NKJV)

Yahweh was the covenant name by which Elohim, the Creator, revealed Himself to His people. This name would connect Him in unbreakable promise to them forever.

The name of Yahweh was so crucial to Jewish worship that devout Jews recited

He is wonderful!

the Shema twice each day: "Hear, O Israel: The LORD our God, the LORD is one!" (Deut. 6:4 NKJV). In fact, it was the first verse taught to Hebrew children. Parents wanted their offspring to hear and confess the name of the Lord before they learned anything else in life.

THE NAME OF A KING

Among all the names given to announce the coming of the Messiah, there are none like the descriptions found in Isaiah 9:6, where the glorious fivefold name of Jesus Christ was recorded seven hundred years before He was born in a lowly manger. The names shone brilliantly against the dark background of a world that had lost its way. Light is come! A Son is given! Isaiah was allowed a look through the telescope of prophecy and saw a new day dawning. God spoke a promise of a new kingdom and a new kind of King, Jesus Christ:

> For unto us a Child is born,
>
> Unto us a Son is given;
>
> And the government will be upon His shoulder.
>
> And His name will be called
>
> Wonderful, Counselor, Mighty God,
>
> Everlasting Father, Prince of Peace. (Isa. 9:6 NKJV)

We must first notice several basics about this prophecy. The words clearly predict that He would be physically birthed; He would become a man in incarnation. It stated, "Unto us a Son is given," and indeed, Jesus was Son of Abraham, Son of David, Son of man, and Son of God.

Furthermore, this Son would be given as a sacrifice. I recall a story from World War

II of a man whose leg had to be amputated. The doctor said to him, "We're going to have to take your leg." The man replied, "No, sir. I am giving my leg for my country." The perspective changes the whole situation. Jesus made His perspective clear when He said, "No one takes My life from Me. I lay it down willingly."

The prophetic verse continues, "The government will be upon His shoulder." All authority would be granted to Him. This Son who was given would rise to become the Regent of the universe. Not only does He have authority over the government of all creation, the planet, and all the ages, but He can be Lord over each individual as well. Jesus would not come to take part in our lives; He would come to take over our lives.

During this season of the year like no other, we should take time to search our hearts and sincerely examine who is on the throne of our will. Every time we try to control our own lives, everything ends up in a mess. Let the government of your own heart be upon Christ's shoulder.

His Name Is Wonderful

Isaiah continued the prophecy, and within the limits of human language, he tried to relate the character of the coming King. Although he used several beautifully vivid terms, the first in the list captures our attention in the most powerful way—the "Wonderful" name of Christ.

Wonderful! Isaiah began his description with this word that comes from the Hebrew people, which refers to supernatural power, something that cannot be explained in terms of human planning. Having Jesus in your life means that it becomes a life filled with wonder and surprise.

In Luke 2:18 (NKJV), we find recorded the response of those who heard the shepherds' report of the birth of Jesus: "All those who heard it marveled at those things which were told them by the shepherds." The excitement of the shepherds was contagious. What a display of marvel and wonder by all those touched by the news of Christ's birth!

A great evangelist early in this century was a man named Rodney "Gypsy"

Smith. It has been estimated that Gypsy made at least forty-seven trips back and forth across the ocean, ministering to multitudes in Europe, Australia, and America. Until the end of his life in 1947, he maintained a glow and an excitement about Jesus that were infectious.

One day, the evangelist was asked how he stayed so fresh in his life and preaching. He replied, "I never lost the wonder!" Gypsy Smith couldn't get over the wonder of being touched by the God of the universe through the salvation given by Jesus Christ. He often said, "I didn't go through colleges and seminaries. They wouldn't have me . . . but I have been to the feet of Jesus."

This old hymn attempts to put the feeling of wonder into words:

> I stand amazed in the presence of Jesus the Nazarene,
>
> And wonder how He could love me,
>
> A sinner, condemned, unclean!
>
> How marvelous! How wonderful!
>
> And my song shall ever be:

How marvelous! How wonderful!

Is my Savior's love for me!

As we look closer at the character of Jesus, there are three areas in which we must exclaim, "He is wonderful!"

Wonderful in His Person

In the Incarnation, God came to earth as a man, placing Himself in a virgin's womb. Can you imagine the God of the universe, cradled in the arms of one of His creation? When the shepherds heard the news of His miraculous birth, they couldn't help spreading the word.

Not only was His birth wondrous, but so was His life. Reflect on these amazing events in His life:

❧ It was just another wedding until Jesus arrived and transformed it into the wedding of the century by turning water into wine. Whatever He touches will change for the better.

Peter and his fishing buddies thought they knew it all and had it all. They would have lived unremarkable lives, but one day they went fishing with Jesus, and they were never the same. No doubt as they watched the nets break under the miraculous catch of fish, they looked at Jesus and exclaimed, "Wonderful! Wonderful!"

Storms were commonplace on the Sea of Galilee, but never was there a night like that one! The disciples found themselves caught in a storm that was about to capsize their boat, so they decided to wake their Master, who was sleeping in the back of the vessel. He simply stood and commanded, "Peace, be still!" They stood in that wet boat looking at a calm sea, and the Scripture says that they were in awe that even the waves and winds obeyed Him.

Jesus could take a common lily and make it as important as a king. He said, "Solomon in all his glory was not arrayed like one of these" (Matt. 6:29 NKJV). He would point at an ordinary sparrow and say, "Don't you wish you had that kind of freedom in your life? You can if you will quit worrying and start trusting Me!"

At the Last Supper, He took common bread and wine, and He gave them a depth of mystery and meaning that we still cannot completely fathom.

Wonderful in His Passion

Jesus was the only human being who ever lived who had the right not to die. "The wages of sin is death," but He knew no sin. When He willingly gave Himself up to the Cross, the rocks rent, the sun hid its light, and the tombs were opened. Jesus bore the sin of the earth on His own body.

We often picture the Christmas story as men seeking after God. "Wise Men Still Seek Him" is a saying that has adorned Christmas cards and tree ornaments for many years now. However, Jesus' arrival on earth was not about man seeking God, but about God seeking man. God desired to make known His life to us and was willing to pay a price to make that happen.

The island of Molokai is one of the Hawaiian Islands. It is famous not as a vacation paradise, but for its history as a place inhabited by a colony of people with leprosy. Years ago, a Catholic priest named Father Damien (born Joseph de Veuster) went there to serve. No one else was willing to take the risk to minister to the unfortunate people. However, the love of Christ called him to that place, and he obeyed, attending to the physical and spiritual needs of the suffering people.

One day, he accidentally spilled boiling water onto his feet, and when he realized he could not feel any pain, he knew that he had succumbed to the deadly disease of leprosy. Later that day as he stepped up to preach in the colony's daily chapel service, he began his address to the men by saying, "My fellow lepers . . ." In that moment, the men recognized that the priest had identified with them, taking their own disease upon himself so that he might minister to them.

Think of your Savior Jesus, who identified with you, taking your sins upon Himself to save you. When I think of the cross and my sinful state that put Jesus upon it, my spirit rises up and cries, "Wonderful! Wonderful!"

Wonderful in His Presence

This wonderful Jesus can live personally in my life and yours. When Jesus comes in,

a new miraculous, supernatural, wonderful dimension comes upon your life.

Jesus loves me for who I am. Too often we become close with people who seem to enjoy being in our presence, only to find out later that they want something from us. Jesus is unselfish in His closeness to us, and His concern is abundant.

I read a story of a man who observed two well-dressed women having dinner in a restaurant. A cake was brought to their table, and because they obviously were celebrating a special occasion, he went over to give his best wishes. "What is the special occasion?" he inquired.

"It is my son's second birthday," said the younger woman.

"Well, where is your son?" asked the man.

The women looked at him in amazement, and the mother replied, "You wouldn't expect me to bring that little brat into a nice place like this, would you?"

Unfortunately, that is how much of our world celebrates the Christmas season—missing the presence of the One who is the source of peace and joy, and who is the very reason for the holiday.

You must grasp this truth—the very moment you invite Jesus Christ into your life, you have a forever Friend. He will never leave you, never forsake you, and He is present at the very moment you need Him in your life.

M O R E   T H A N   W O N D E R F U L

As we have seen, had Isaiah included only the name "Wonderful" in the prophetic verse, it would have imparted more about Jesus' character than we could fully absorb. But Isaiah could not stop there. With the all-encompassing name "Wonderful" ringing in our souls, let us learn more about the coming King.

He Is Counselor—He Comes Along Beside Us

Today many siren voices are luring us away from the Lord's will. The psalmist warned,

Blessed is the man

Who walks not in the counsel of the ungodly,

Nor stands in the path of sinners,

Nor sits in the seat of the scornful. (Ps. 1:1 NKJV)

In fact, often we cannot trust even the counsels of our own hearts; as Jeremiah said, "The heart is deceitful" (Jer. 17:9 NKJV). However, in our wonderful Lord, I know immediately I have a Counselor who meets all the qualifications for supplying my need.

My Counselor has put His thoughts in writing. He has given me sixty-six books containing His wisdom and promises. He is an Author with the highest credentials, and every word He has ever written was composed to correct, comfort, and cheer me. The psalmist rejoiced again and again over this special provision in Psalm 119 (NKJV):

Your word is a lamp to my feet
And a light to my path. (v. 105)

The entrance of Your words gives light;
It gives understanding to the simple. (v. 130)

Direct my steps by Your word,
And let no iniquity have dominion over me. (v. 133)

Your word is very pure;
Therefore Your servant loves it. (v. 140)

I rejoice at Your word

As one who finds great treasure. (v. 162)

Bernice Peyman recorded her love for God's written Word in these classic lines:

Though its cover is worn

And its pages are torn

And in places are traces of tears,

Yet more precious than gold

Is this Book worn and old

That shatters and scatters my fears.

When I prayerfully look

In this precious old Book

And my eyes scan the pages I see

Many tokens of love

From the Father above

Who is nearest and dearest to me.

This old Book is my guide

'Tis a friend by my side

It will lighten and brighten my way

And each promise I find

Soothes and gladdens my mind

As I read it and heed it each day.

This Counselor understands me. After all, He was in all points tested as we are, "yet without sin" (Heb. 4:15 NKJV). He "knows our frame . . . that we are dust" (Ps. 103:14 NKJV). I don't have to explain my hurt, my pain, my motives, or my fears and failures—He knows them all. Despite that knowledge, my Counselor came and died for my sins. He knows who I am, but He still makes Himself available to me, today and every day, to bear my burdens. He promised to never leave me or forsake me, and He has never broken that promise.

When I think of the presence of Jesus, I go back to an event that took place when I was fourteen. At that time my father was still struggling with alcohol, screaming and hollering at my mother, and calling her names. During one of his confrontations, I stepped right between them, and I said, "You are not going to talk to my mother like that."

Dad did not appreciate my interference, and picking up a glass bowl, he broke it over my head, shouting, "Get out! You aren't going to live here anymore!"

Well, I left—ran down the street, under a bypass, onto the railroad tracks, and climbed up on the old trestle where all of the boys used to gather. I sat up on that trestle and looked over the edge.

I thought, *I can either jump or just sit here until a train comes, but I am staying until something happens. I don't have any place to go.*

Then the Voice, the One who has always been there, began to speak to my spirit, saying, *Son . . .* You see, He always calls me "son" when He wants to nurture me a bit. He said, *Son, you get up off this trestle and start walking back toward the road, and I'll take care of you.* I didn't know what that meant, but feeling His presence, I obeyed.

Before long, a good friend of mine came along and called out, "Ronnie, your mom is worried about you." When I replied that I was fine, he said, "You are going to stay at my place a couple of nights until everything settles down. Everything is going to be fine."

Well, it was. I am alive and here today. I have lived long enough to see my daddy touched by Jesus, and I later had the privilege of laying my hands on his head as he was ordained as a deacon.

At every juncture of my life, when I look back through the pain of that experience, the main emotion that overwhelms me is wonder, for Jesus was unmistakably at my side when I needed Him. He is truly a wonderful Counselor!

He Is Mighty God—He Gives Courage for Living

Our wonderful Lord came to this world to take on our enemies:

Who is this King of glory?
The LORD strong and mighty,

The LORD mighty in battle.

(Ps. 24:8 NKJV)

This reference reveals the fact that God is a conquering hero; He is champion over every foe.

Jesus conquered life, facing its temptations and tests. He came out of the ivory palaces to do battle for our souls. Hebrews 2:10, 14–15 (NKJV) tells how our Captain of Salvation accomplished His mission:

> It was fitting for Him, for whom are all things and by whom are all things, in bringing many sons to glory, to make the captain of their salvation perfect through sufferings . . . Inasmuch then as the children have partaken of flesh and blood, He Himself likewise shared in the same, that through death He might destroy him who had the power of death, that is, the devil, and release those who through fear of death were all their lifetime subject to bondage.

By His death, our wonderful Lord destroyed the power of death by which Satan enslaved us. The mighty God came to deliver us from the chains of the enemy. Jesus warred on our behalf in the dark regions, but on the third day, He arose triumphant. He conquered death, leaving its scepter and crown shattered in an empty tomb, and broke down its gates, so we never have to fear death's sting. His victory is ours to claim in our daily walk. The enemy cannot reach us as we stand in the center of His power and authority.

He Is Everlasting Father—He Gives Tender Care

In the Old Testament, we find very few references to God as a Father to us. One of the great truths that Jesus came to impart to us was the concept of God as Father of all who believe, for when we turn past the pages of the Old Testament and leaf through the Gospels, we find more than 150 references to God as our Father.

Jesus taught us to direct our prayers to the Father in the model prayer. He instructed, "In this manner, therefore, pray: Our Father in heaven, hallowed be Your name" (Matt. 6:9 NKJV). He wanted us to learn to seek the Father's face.

Christ clearly knew His mission and calling while here on earth: to declare to a lost world the name of the loving Father. He fulfilled this mission, as we read in His prayer for us, "I have declared to them Your name, and will declare it, that the love with which You loved Me may be in them, and I in them" (John 17:26 NKJV).

When Jesus spoke of God as Father, it was in the best sense of the word. In today's cold world, we often find fathers who are abusive or neglectful, unloving and irresponsible. The "Everlasting Father" is not like these poor representatives of parenthood. His attention to me is limitless, watching over His child with loving provision and concern. As Father, His name signifies protection. The same God who rules the vastness of eternity, whose life stretches from before the beginning of time to beyond the end of our present earth, cares for me as a Father does a son.

Because we are a part of His family, you and I take on great significance. He has numbered the hairs on your head. He rejoices when one child repents. He would stop if just one of His children touched the hem of His garment in faith. Augustine once rejoiced, "He loves us every one as though there were but one of us to love."

Jesus wanted us to know that the Father was not impersonal, imposing upon us a ritualistic, dead religion. As a Father, God desires a relationship with us that is warm and loving. In Paul's letter to the Romans, we read these astounding verses: "For as many as are led by the Spirit of God, these are sons of God. For you did not receive the spirit of bondage again to fear, but you received the Spirit of adoption by whom we cry out, 'Abba, Father'" (Rom. 8:14–15 NKJV). He is our eternal Abba.

Since God is our Father, our suffering is not borne alone, and suffering comes to us for a reason. I remember when my daughter, Heather, was an infant, her tear ducts were blocked. We had to hold Heather down while the doctors performed a painful procedure to open those ducts. I'm sure in her little baby mind, she had serious doubts about the necessity of that ordeal. Yet as her parents, we knew it had to be done so that the health of her eyes could be preserved. She was hurt in order to be healed. Our loving Father knows that at times His corrective hand must intervene so that future failure and pain can be averted.

Perhaps the most wonderful aspect of our relationship with the Father is the forgiveness that is ours. One of the greatest stories Jesus told while on earth was that of the prodigal son. So often we study the young boy's failure in the parable, but the truth is that it presents the story of a loving father. Consider his qualities as related in Luke 15:

- He was generous (v. 12).

- He exercised tough love (vv. 13–16).

- He was honest in business (v. 17).

- He was watching and waiting patiently for his child (v. 20).

- He was openly emotional and loving (v. 20).

- He understood without having to be told (v. 21).

- He was eager to forgive and restore (v. 22).

- He knew how to celebrate (vv. 23–25).

Each of these qualities represents my everlasting Father. The God of the universe is Father to me, and no human relationship can equal the bond that He seals between His child and Himself. What a wonderful Father!

He Is Prince of Peace—He Gives Calmness in Life's Storms

Isaiah closed his list of descriptive names with a name filled with hope. Jesus is the very embodiment of peace. The Old Testament word for "peace" is *shalom*. It means more than the absence of hostilities; it indicates the abundant provision of everything a person needs.

Some think peace involves quietness. Some think it is like a graveyard. Others think the face of a sleeping infant perfectly relays the sense of peace. None of these truly capture the word. Peace is not silence, death, or innocence. Rather, peace is the wonderful sense of calmness and well-being that fills our lives no matter how loud, difficult, or confusing things may be.

To attain this peace, we must sign a treaty of surrender. Long ago, in the councils of eternity, Truth and Mercy had a meeting: "Mercy and truth have met together; righteousness and peace have kissed" (Ps. 85:10 NKJV). Can you imagine the agenda of that meeting? Perhaps Truth spoke up and said, "Those humans—they are all sinners; they don't deserve to be saved, and they shouldn't live in peace." As his proof text, Truth read Isaiah 48:22 (NKJV), "'There is no peace,' says the LORD, 'for the wicked.'"

Mercy could no longer keep silent and proclaimed, "Listen, Truth, the Prince of Peace wants to save mankind! Look at Isaiah 53:5 (NKJV). It says, 'But He was wounded for our transgressions, He was bruised for our iniquities; the chastisement for our peace was upon Him, and by His stripes we are healed.'" Mercy continued with yet another text, "Therefore, having been justified by faith, we have peace with God through our Lord Jesus Christ" (Rom. 5:1 NKJV).

As Mercy lifted high the signed treaty of a man's surrendered heart, Mercy won, and Jesus planted a kiss of righteousness upon that soul, saving him eternally.

The influence of the Prince of Peace can grow as we allow Jesus to govern every part of our lives. The more we struggle to maintain control on our own, the less peace we will have in our hearts. When we trust God, His peace stands guard over our lives. Isaiah wrote,

You will keep him in perfect peace,

Whose mind is stayed on You,

Because he trusts in You. (Isa. 26:3 NKJV)

This peace is our fortune to share with others. Isaiah must have felt the joy of being the bearer of such a wonderful message when he penned these words:

How beautiful upon the mountains

Are the feet of him who brings good news,

Who proclaims peace,

Who brings glad tidings of good things,

Who proclaims salvation,

Who says to Zion,

"Your God reigns!" (Isa. 52:7 NKJV)

BEYOND WORDS

When I have expressed everything I can possibly express to you, and I have exhausted the capacity of language that is in my spirit to say, I have not told you one-millionth of how wonderful the Savior is! My heart can only echo the powerful hymn:

O, for a thousand tongues to sing my great Redeemer's praise,

The glories of my God and King, the triumphs of His grace.

Hear Him, ye deaf; His praise, ye dumb, your loosened tongues employ;

Ye blind, behold your Savior come; and leap, ye lame, for joy.

During this season, I invite you to come to the One who, when you are on the top of the world, is right there, saying, "Good! Go for it!" I urge you to embrace the One who, when you are at your lowest point, says, "Come with Me. When you walk through the valley of the shadow of death, you will fear no evil! I will be with you, child!"

You see, His shoulders are wide enough to carry not only the governments of the universe, but also your many burdens. If life has lost its mystery and wonder, look to the One who is wonderful. If you don't know what to do next in life, reach out to your Counselor. If you have no earthly parent or if you experienced abuse and mistreatment, place your pain in the arms of the everlasting Father who cares for you. If your god is too small, rise up and meet the One who is mighty God. And if your life is torn with turmoil, rest in the One who is the Prince of Peace.

What a wonderful Savior! 🎵

Christmas Declares Our Value

{ JOHN BEVERE

Christmas is viewed many different ways. Through the eyes of many young children, it is when Santa Claus brings toys. Older children enjoy a carefree break from school as well as a chance to get desired gifts. Parents often dread the holidays as a time of shopping, stress, and debt. For retail employees, the season brings long hours. To merchants, it yields end-of-the-year profits. Amid all this chaos, most still remember it as a special family time. For some, the memories are bittersweet as they remember the absence of loved ones. { But what is Christmas to Christians? I believe this season highlights our value to our loving and gracious heavenly Father. Take this moment and think about your worth. As we wander through various shops this season, we see price tags that display the assigned value of the items they represent. Some prices are inexpensive; others are costly, varying accordingly with their value and importance. As wise shoppers, we are careful never to pay more than what an item is worth. We comparison shop until we are certain we will get our money's worth.

Everything has some sort of value. This value is determined by the eye of the purchaser. We'd never pay more than what something was worth to us. When Mark McGwire hit his seventieth home run in 1998 and subsequently set the major-league record for most home runs hit in a single season, the ball sold for $2.7 million, and the article I read said some were willing to pay more for it. Personally, I would never have paid that amount. First, I don't have that much money, and second— and most important—it doesn't mean that much to me. To the person who made the purchase, the value

of that ball was at least $2.7 million. If it wasn't, he would not have bought it.

HOW CAN WE FIND TRUE VALUE?

Can we find our true value through our society? No, the value of a human life varies tremendously, even within the borders of this great nation. Millions of children are being killed before they are born because their lives are inconveniences to their parents. They are considered better dead than alive, and others are paid to sweep their tiny lives away. Yet these parents are acting in accordance with the politicians and voters who have enacted laws that do not value life.

Husbands and fathers abandon wives and children, forsaking the very relationships they vowed to nourish and protect. They no longer value these relationships as worth fighting for, afraid they might cost too much time and effort to repair. Consequently, they place their comfort and pleasure above those of their loved ones. Broken homes produce millions of wounded and frightened people who seriously doubt their value.

The scenarios vary, from the deep despair of women in houses of prostitution where intimacies are sold for a few dollars, to power drug dealers who sell substances with the ability to destroy the lives of their customers. Then there are doctors willing to assist people in suicide for a fee and greedy businessmen who take advantage of vulnerable households. The list goes on and on.

What mankind values in one generation, it resents in the next. Given such inconsistencies in our culture, we need an enduring standard. What about God? How does He value us? As our Creator, He alone determines our true value. God, not man, establishes the real measure of worth in this universe, for "what is highly valued among men is detestable in God's sight" (Luke 16:15 NIV). Jesus questioned, "What profit is it to a man if he gains the whole world, and loses his own soul? Or what will a man give in exchange for his soul?" (Matt. 16:26 NKJV).

Consider for a moment all the wealth in this world. Envision not one, but all of the multimillion-dollar mansions and the nations that hold them. Add to that every gem and ounce of precious metal. Include in the sum the total of fine cars, boats, planes, and state-of-the-art electronics—just to mention some of the nicer items.

So much treasure exists on this globe that it is almost unimaginable. This world's assets produce a gross world product of approximately 35.8 trillion U.S. dollars (that is $35,800,000,000,000). That is a lot of wealth! Men have stolen, killed, lied, cheated, and gambled for a fraction of that wealth, yet Jesus tells us that a man who exchanges himself for all this world offers has made an unprofitable deal.

WHAT ONE MAN IS WORTH

When I was in my early twenties, I worked for a wealthy couple. One of my responsibilities was making sure the vehicles were serviced, and that often involved driving their cars. At one point while driving their top-of-the-line Mercedes-Benz through an affluent area in Dallas, I had to stop for road construction. As I waited, I couldn't help noticing a particular construction worker. His jeans were filthy and full of holes. His hair and beard were scraggly and covered with the dust of his labor. No part of him was clean, and his features were chiseled with hardship. I watched him intently as he labored.

Suddenly, I heard the Lord whisper, "John, do you know that man is worth more to Me than the car you are driving?" I looked about me and breathed in the fresh, clean scent of the car that surrounded me in luxury. I let my mind wander to how it appeared and appealed to others as the very symbol of success. Then I glanced again at the worn and dirty man.

I heard His voice again: "Do you know this man is worth more to Me than that building?" My attention shifted to the exclusive high-rise condominium that loomed before me. Only the wealthy could afford its prestigious address. It was sleek, modern, and surrounded by elaborate landscaping.

I thought again of the many who might "ooh" and "aah" over the car I sat in or at the chance to live in such a pricey condominium. I imagined them running toward these luxuries while passing this dirty man without a second glance.

Again I heard the Holy Spirit whisper to my heart, "That man is worth more than all the finest cars and expensive buildings this world can offer." My attention was riveted because, until then, I had known this mentally only in terms of information. I had even repeated something to this effect when I witnessed to others, but now I saw it in a different light. Through this man, God was attempting to change my perspective of each individual's importance in His eyes.

If our true worth is more than all the wealth of the world, then what accurately reflects our value? Christmas is a revelation of our true worth. The Bible says, "For God so loved the world that He gave His only begotten Son" (John 3:16 NKJV). Through the betrayal of Adam, we were brought under servitude to the wicked king, Lucifer (Luke 4:6). By Adam's disobedience, we were made slaves to sin. As the lord of sin, Lucifer had legal claim to us and refused to give us up. We were destined for eternal darkness and powerless to liberate ourselves from the clutches of sin. The only way we could be free was for God to be willing to purchase us back.

Our sin was so grievous and far reaching that we could not be ransomed by any wealth of this earthly creation. In answer to our hopelessness God gave of Himself, His only Son, Jesus, as a ransom for us. God tells us,

Those who trust in their wealth

And boast in the multitude of their riches,

None of them can by any means redeem his brother,

Nor give to God a ransom for him—

For the redemption of their souls is costly. (Ps. 49:6–8 NKJV)

Our souls are worth so much that our freedom could be purchased only by Jesus Himself. Paul told us, "God bought you with a high price" (1 Cor. 6:20 NLT), and He "is so rich in kindness that he purchased our freedom through the blood of his Son" (Eph. 1:7 NLT).

There is no person or thing God values in this universe more than Jesus, yet God valued us enough to send His most beloved Son. If God did not highly value you, He would never have given the life of Jesus in exchange for yours. Now here is the amazing reality of what He did. Allow me to put it in financial terms to make it easier to understand. If we were worth one cent less to God than the value of Jesus, then He would never have given Him for us. God is wise and would never make such an unprofitable

purchase. An unprofitable purchase occurs when something of great value is given for something of less value. Jesus Himself affirmed this when He prayed just before His death: "Then the world will know that you sent me and will understand that you love them as much as you love me" (John 17:23 NLT). Wow! Do you see how important you are to God? Can you glimpse the greatness of His love for you? Christmas declares your true value to God!

W H O   A M   I ?

Some may say, "Yes, God did that for all of mankind, but who am I among so many?" In answer to that question, I believe if you were the only one, He still would have paid the same price for you. We see this in an episode during Jesus' ministry. He had spent an entire day teaching the multitude about the kingdom of God. He was physically exhausted, yet there was an important mission that could not wait. Under the direction of the Holy Spirit, Jesus boarded a boat, told the disciples to cross the Sea of Galilee, and collapsed into a deep sleep. In the midst of the sea a storm arose that threatened their lives, but Jesus was so tired, He remained sound asleep. In despera-

tion, the disciples awoke Him to tell of their grave danger. Jesus rose and commanded the waves and wind to be still.

After a good portion of the night was spent crossing a troubled sea, the group
reached the other side. Maybe there, away from the crowds, they could find some rest.
But no sooner had they left their boat than they were met by a violent man full of
demons. The wild man lived among the tombs and was so completely possessed, he
could not be restrained by men or chains: "All day long and throughout the night, he
would wander among the tombs and in the hills, screaming and hitting himself with
stones" (Mark 5:3–5 NLT).

If this man were alive today, he would be placed in a mental institution in solitary
confinement. He would probably receive shock treatments. He certainly would be considered a social outcast, one kept alive only because of pity and because the law would
not permit him to be put to rest. To most people, he would represent a worthless drain
on society. His life would be one void of value.

Yet Jesus, the Father, and the Spirit of God saw him differently. Jesus ministered to him in a powerful way, and so mighty was his deliverance that before day's end, he was seated next to Jesus, clothed, and in his right mind. Now here is the amazing part. After Jesus ministered to that one lone, tormented individual, He left and "crossed over again by boat to the other side" (Mark 5:21 NKJV). I'll never forget the day God showed me this. I was awed by the compassion of Jesus. Though exhausted from a long, hard day, He crossed the sea and fought a storm just to minister to the outcast man, then He got into the boat and went all the way back to the other side again. He went to great lengths to ease the suffering and torment of one man. Do you see the value God places on just one individual?

Jesus told a parable that reinforces our individual importance and worth to God:

> If you had one hundred sheep, and one of them strayed away and was lost in the wilderness, wouldn't you leave the ninety-nine others to go and search for the lost one until you found it? And then you would joyfully carry it home on your shoulders. When you arrived, you would call together your friends and neighbors

to rejoice with you because your lost sheep was found. In the same way, heaven will be happier over one lost sinner who returns to God than over ninety-nine others who are righteous and haven't strayed away! (Luke 15:4–7 NLT)

If you were the only one lost who needed to be ransomed, He still would have come for you.

WHAT IS YOUR INDIVIDUAL WORTH?

I had been a Christian only a few years when the Lord spoke something that revolutionized my thinking. I was in prayer when I heard Him whisper, "John, do you know that I esteem you more important than Myself?"

I remember my initial reaction to those words. What a blasphemous and utterly presumptuous thought, not to mention irreverent! I almost blurted out, "Get behind me, Satan."

Although deep in my heart I sensed it was God's voice, I still responded with questioning disbelief, "Lord Jesus, this is too far-out for me to believe. It seems blasphemous to believe that You, who created the heavens and earth, would consider me—John Bevere, a mere man—more important than Yourself. The only way I will be able to accept such a thought is if You give me three New Testament Scriptures to prove what I think I just heard from You."

I sensed His pleasure that I wanted these witnesses from His Word, and I immediately heard in my heart, "What does Philippians 2:3 say?"

The passage was familiar, so I quoted it aloud: "Let nothing be done through selfish ambition or conceit, but in lowliness of mind let each esteem others better than himself" (NKJV).

The Lord said, "You have your first Scripture."

I argued, "Lord, that is Paul speaking to the Philippian believers, telling them to esteem others better than themselves. That does not refer to Your relationship with me."

In reply I heard the Lord say, "Son, I never tell My children to do anything that I don't do Myself!" Then He showed me that this is the problem in many homes. Parents

expect behavior from their children that they themselves do not exhibit. For example, they tell their children not to fight, but they do so themselves and then wonder why their children don't obey them. However, the Lord never expects anything from us that He doesn't do Himself.

I agreed to this point, but still had some doubts: "Lord, I still need two more Scriptures."

He then asked a question that riveted my heart: "John, who hung on the cross, Me or you?"

I said soberly, "You did, Jesus."

"It should have been you hanging on that cross," He said, "but I hung on it bearing your sins, judgment, sickness, disease, pain, and poverty. I did it because I esteemed you better than Myself."

I trembled as I heard His words. All doubt was eradicated by what He had spoken. I soberly thought to myself, *He did not deserve any bit of what He got. He was righteous and innocent.*

Then 1 Peter 2:24 (NKJV) came to my heart: "Who Himself bore our sins in His own body on the tree, that we, having died to sins, might live for righteousness—by whose stripes you were healed."

I knew then that He truly considered me more important than Himself. I felt as though I had glimpsed a whole other dimension of His love for me. I felt tears trickle down my face as I began to worship Him. I already knew there would be a third verse. "What does Romans 12:10 say?" I heard in my heart.

Again it was another familiar Scripture, one I was able to quote, "Be kindly affectionate to one another with brotherly love, in honor giving preference to one another" (NKJV). I sensed Him questioning me, "Am I not the firstborn of many brethren? I prefer My brothers and sisters because I esteem them better than Myself."

I had heard that Jesus loved me many times before, but when He spoke those words to my heart, His love was so real that it became a part of me. He loves each of us individually and uniquely. He calls those who love and obey Him "His treasures." A treasure is something that is valued as special and worth protecting. He calls each of us the apple of His eye. And—if you can grasp this—He rejoices over us!

The angels are confused as they look on. They compare us with the majesty they behold in the presence of a glorious and holy God and wonder why He gives us such attention. They wonder why He is so mindful of us. They have heard how His thoughts of love and goodness toward us cannot be numbered, for they are greater in number than the sands of the oceans. They see that we are His prized possessions, His sought-out jewels, the living stones, who build up the tabernacle in which He has always desired to dwell.

Why would God feel this way toward us? What have we done to deserve such love? The amazing truth is, we've done nothing! Nothing we could do comes close to meriting His love. For when we were lost, decrepit sinners—and even enemies—He sent His Son to die for us. He saw in us what only His love could see. He saw treasures in the midst of corruption, sin, and depravity. He viewed as precious what many would consider worthless or of little value. He looked beyond our present state and saw what only His grace could produce.

This truth lends a greater understanding of this verse: "God purchased you at a high price. Don't be enslaved by the world" (1 Cor. 7:23 NLT). Why would anyone who has experienced such love and value want to return to the filth that once enslaved him?

"He gave his life to purchase freedom for everyone. This is the message that God gave to the world at the proper time" (1 Tim. 2:6 NLT). This is the true message of Christmas. It was given the night the hosts of heaven came to earth to declare, "Glory to God in the highest heaven, and peace on earth to all whom God favors" (Luke 2:14 NLT).

This Christmas, as you browse through the stores buying gifts for loved ones, remember the unfathomable value that God places on you and everyone who is called by His name. ❧

Celebrate the Gift of Worship

❧ JACKIE McCULLOUGH

Jesus was born in the fourth monarchy of Rome, when Rome was at its peak. During that time, Augustus Caesar was ruler, and the Roman Empire was a major world power. The Romans had accomplished some great things, establishing roadways to enable people to travel within the Roman Empire and developing one monetary system to promote commerce. That was the world situation as it awaited the advent of Jesus Christ. ❧ Of course, the Roman government did not know that it was playing a part in the unfolding of the fulfillment of prophecy, but that's how God works. He uses politics, economics, and social and cultural changes to prepare the world for the expression and demonstration of His supernatural power. We are in that kind of upheaval now. Happenings in the White House and the federal government point to God's intent to move mightily among us.

During that time, Judea became a tributary, was supervised politically by the army of the Roman government, and paid taxes under its rule. The Roman government levied heavy taxes and mandated censuses. Yet all of that was part of God's plan, for the Bible says that Joseph and Mary, while she was with child and about to deliver, were required to go to Bethlehem of Judea, according to the law and decree of Augustus Caesar.

The purpose was to pay taxes and register in the census so that Caesar would know how many people were in his empire and how many men he could recruit for his army. The census was done according to the lineage of the family, which was important because it had been declared that a woman would have a baby in the lineage of David. According to the prophecy, "'They shall call His name Immanuel,' which is translated, 'God with us'" (Matt. 1:23 NKJV). It became part of the historical record that Jesus was born into a particular family. That could not be refuted historically because it was the fulfillment of prophecy.

As it happened to Joseph and Mary, when the government flexes its muscles and you experience inconveniences, it is easy to conclude that the government is calling the shots. But that is not true. God is moving in your circumstances, and you may have to relocate, change jobs, or experience a time of great upheaval to arrive at His desired destination.

THE WORD IS BEING FULFILLED

Mary, heavy with child, found herself riding on a donkey. If you've ever ridden a donkey, you know that it's not a comfortable, cushioned ride. It's not like riding in a Lexus or a BMW. Imagine being heavy with child and riding many miles with the baby resting on your pelvis in the final stages of pregnancy. Yet despite all the hardships, it was the fulfillment of prophecy. No matter what may be happening to you, the Word of God is being fulfilled in your life. If He said it, even in the midst of hardships, He is going to bring it to pass.

Joseph and Many came to the appointed place set by the government, but they could not find a comfortable place for Mary to have her child. Remember, her pregnancy was not her desire or wish. She didn't raise her hand and say, "I want to be." The Lord chose her, an ordinary young girl minding her own business, preparing to get married, planning on having an ordinary family. You know—you try to be ordinary and pursue a typical life, and God interrupts all of your plans. You try to have a traditional, humdrum family, and God, in the midst of hardship, unfolds His purpose. God interrupted Mary's plans, raised question marks over her life, and made her look as if she were pregnant with an illegitimate child. But in the midst of it, God's word was that this child would be the Savior of the world.

When Joseph and Mary reached Bethlehem, you would have thought the innkeepers would have recognized she was a special woman and made room for her at the inn. You'd think they would have given her an opportunity to at least have her baby in comfort. Instead, she had Him in a common way. It seems that when God uses you, He takes you the rough way. When you're slated for greatness, there is almost

always a lot of discomfort. It seems that everyone else can ride easy, but you've got to go the difficult way. It seems that whenever God has His hands heavy on you, nothing comes easily. When you envy the folks who have it easy, recognize that they are going nowhere. Nothing comes easily to those who are slated for greatness.

The Bible says Mary laid Him in a manger. A manger is a feeding trough designed to hold feed or fodder for livestock. She wrapped Jesus in swaddling cloths, which are narrow strips of cloth wrapped around an infant to restrict movement. Even though He

was born in a stable, a remote place that was not fashionable, a place where kings and persons of means would not be born, His mother cared for Him in a way to ensure that He would grow and develop normally. In spite of the adverse conditions, she gave Him the best care she could.

There was great political upheaval as people came from everywhere to pay taxes and be registered in the census. The government was flexing its muscles, with Augustus Caesar looking for more political power. The poor family was a part of the political process, caught up in the quagmire of trying to pay dues owed to society.

While Mary gave birth to her baby in a stable, wrapped Him in swaddling cloths, and laid Him in the manger in the midst of the animals, something supernatural was happening. God was fulfilling prophecy to make sure that all the prophet's words would come to pass. Jesus was to be born in Bethlehem of Judea, not in Nazareth. If it takes Augustus Caesar to get Him there, so be it. If it takes paying taxes to get Him there, it's all right. Sometimes God has to inconvenience you to get you where He wants you to go. Sometimes God has to make things happen to push you out of your corner to get you to where He wants you. Sometimes God must close one door and open another in order to move you into your ordained path. God is constantly weaving and unfolding His master plan, and sooner or later, you will see the glory and majesty of God's plan.

GOD SPEAKS TO THOSE WHO NEED HIM

The biblical account of the Christmas story says that at the time of His birth, there was a sound from heaven, and a messenger came out of heaven—not to kings or high priests,

Pharisees or scribes—but to the people who had the lowliest occupation, the shepherds. To be a shepherd did not mean you were high on the totem pole. It meant you belonged in the lower-income bracket. But when God was ready to announce the Christmas story, He went to the lower-income folks. He didn't go to the high-income or middle-income group. He found men who were of meager means. Many of us are struggling to be high-income individuals, and that is why we miss what God is saying. He speaks to those of us who need Him to come by and make a difference in our lives. You are a candidate for supernatural intervention!

The shepherds were ordinary people, but they were men who were occupied with their duties. God seeks to reveal Himself to people who are occupied, those who are taking care of business. They were taking care of the sheep by night. They weren't sleeping on the job. They were alert and had a divine encounter while they were doing something, engaged in their occupation and assignment. It might not have been a fancy assignment, but they were busy, not loafing around somewhere. They were not just sitting around doing nothing.

While the shepherds were diligently performing a humble task, the Bible says that an angel appeared to them and said, "Fear not" (Luke 2:10 KJV). The Church is not used to supernatural intervention. Many of you would be afraid if the Lord should move in a mighty way. As soon as you raise your hands and the Holy Spirit starts to take you out of yourself, you pull back. When a heavy anointing comes upon the Church, you stop praising and sit down because you are not familiar with supernatural expression. Some of you are afraid of getting lost in the Holy Spirit or being "slain in the Spirit." Some are afraid of God's opening up the heavens and calling them by name. But I hear God saying, "Fear not! I've got something to tell you. Fear not! I've got something to show you."

We are afraid of the supernatural. We're afraid of God's revealing Himself in a new and powerful way, but as long as we can keep control with just a little clapping here and there, we'll walk out empty. We enter our churches and go through dry services, trying to make something happen when nothing is happening. God wants to come where you are, open up the heavens, and give you a preview. The apostle Paul wrote,

Eye has not seen, nor ear heard,

Nor have entered into the heart of man

The things which God has prepared for those who love Him. (1 Cor. 2:9 NKJV)

DON'T BE AFRAID

An angel appeared suddenly to the shepherds and said, "Don't be afraid." The angel had to say the same thing to Mary, Zacharias, and Joseph: "Don't be afraid." I am saying the same thing to the Church: "Don't be afraid." Don't be afraid of God's calling you. Don't be afraid of God's speaking to you. Don't be afraid of God's revealing Himself. We're always waiting for somebody to give us a word, but God Himself wants to speak to you. God wants to reveal and unveil Himself. So, "fear not."

The angel came, and the glory of the Lord shone round about them. The glory of the Lord is the presence of the Lord. Many of us are afraid of His presence. When the praises go up and the presence of God is manifested, you often see people looking around at one another. They may get a little happy and then sit down or fight to hold themselves back. They say, "Hallelujah," but as soon as they feel the "hallelujah" taking over, they swallow it back down because they are afraid of the presence of God.

In God's presence there is fullness, and at His right hand there are pleasures forevermore. In the presence of God I abandon my insecurities and gain confidence. In the presence of God my mind is open to illumination and inspiration. He takes away the dullness and dryness and turns the light on my life. In the presence of God I get clarity and direction, and He loosens the shackles and sets me free.

The presence of the Lord was revealed to the shepherds, and they were afraid. They had never experienced something supernatural before, yet the angel said to them, "Do not be afraid." This Christmas season, do not be afraid of the supernatural. In a season like this, God often speaks clearly to give people direction.

We must worship God as King. We must put Jesus first. This is His birthday. He is the honored guest, but we have allowed buying gifts in the name of Santa Claus, cooking, and eating to replace Him. We don't see, hear, or receive anything in this season because we're not in the presence of the Lord. We reject His presence and are caught up with the commercialization of Christmas—too busy trying to impress, too busy trying to be like the world and run after the advertised goods of the world, too busy getting involved in "churchy" things. We celebrate around Jesus, and we celebrate about Jesus, but we don't celebrate Jesus. We use the name of Jesus to get, but we're empty and come out of our situations without direction because we're not celebrating Jesus.

GOOD TIDINGS OF GREAT JOY

God never sends a messenger empty-handed. When God sends an angel, he brings a message. The angel said, "Fear not: for, behold, I bring you good tidings of great joy" (Luke 2:10 KJV). The angel was the first to bring the gospel message of good tidings. Jesus is the gospel. Without Jesus there is no gospel. Those of us who are redeemed and washed in the blood of the Lamb can cry out to others, "I bring you good tidings of great joy!"

This season we must no longer preach messages couched in depression. When dysfunctional preachers share their emotional problems in the midst of Christmas, they make us depressed because they're depressed. But this is not a season to be depressed.

The drunkard, the sinner, the whoremonger, and the liar are the ones who are depressed. But Christians, in spite of circumstances, should celebrate who Jesus is. We must not get into the pulpit and talk as if we do not have a Savior. Jesus came to rebuke depression and bring good tidings. Your home may be about to break up, but I bring you good tidings. You may not see a way out of your circumstances, but I bring you good tidings: God will make a way!

The problem is, we're not ready to receive these good tidings because we are afraid of what's happening to us and what God is doing. We don't understand a lot of things that God does, so we reject them. Don't be afraid of what you see. Don't be afraid of what you're experiencing right now. In the midst of it there are good tidings. This is the season when God brings you something. Look to God. This is the season when God wants to give you good tidings of great joy—good news.

Geographically, Palestine is sandwiched between Egypt and Syria, so the Roman Empire, which conquered all that area, also conquered Palestine. The Jews had no army or political leader of their own. They were subjected to the Roman Empire, and their only ruling bodies were their Sanhedrin court, their synagogues, and the Mosaic Law. The people were under Roman power. Previously, they were under the power of Greek and Medo-Persian Empires, and before them, the Jews were under Babylonian rule. They had been passed politically from one power to another, but in the midst of that political mess Jesus was coming. He came to the Jews first because the Bible says, "He came to His own, and His own did not receive Him" (John 1:11 NKJV).

Do not be distracted by what you see and hear. When politicians cut the budget and make changes in the federal government, many people are affected. Look at the post office, the immigration office, and any other bureaucracy. Most of the people are shuffling paper and paper clips, with one person licking a stamp, another posting a stamp, and another mailing. We're all caught up in bureaucracy, not a thinking job or one with any identity. Just pushing paper and getting a check. That's the way plantations were run, so when they got ready to close the plantations down, there was nowhere for people to go. But God is saying in the midst of all of this, "I bring you good tidings of great joy." Not just a little bit of joy. When God does what He wants to do, it's joy unspeakable and full of glory. The half has never been told! For unto you common people, unto you ordinary people, is born in the City of David a Savior, an Emancipator, a Liberator.

God can handle anything. God can turn around anything happening in the White House. God can fix anything going on in your house. We must rebuke the spirit of the world that comes to steal our joy and distract us from the true meaning of Christmas. We must celebrate Christmas within the context of the Word of God. Jesus is Christ the Messiah, Christ the Shining One, the Lord.

THIS SHALL BE A SIGN

"And this shall be a sign unto you" (Luke 2:12 KJV). The angel of the Lord was conveying, "I'm not playing with your mind. This is a supernatural manifestation, but I know that because you're human, you need a sign." The angels came down to convince

the shepherds that this was not a phantom, a ghost, or a figment of the imagination. The Christmas story is a reality. This is not *Miracle on 34th Street* where you must make up a Santa Claus. This is not a classic movie. We're talking about Jesus, who came to become the Savior of the world.

"And this shall be a sign unto you." When Jesus came, He brought signs. So in the middle of the Christmas celebration, look for signs. Look for direction. Expect God to show you things you haven't seen before. When you take your family to church on Christmas, say, "God, show me a sign. I need direction about things happening in my family. I need to know what to do and how to do it. I'm tired of being beaten up by the system and the economy. As I worship, celebrate, and give You the honor and praise, make it clear. God, give me light in the midst of darkness. God, lift up my hung-down head. Make my crooked paths straight, and remove any stumbling blocks."

"And this shall be a sign unto you." In the midst of announcing, pronouncing, and proclaiming the Christmas story and the coming of Jesus, our children must learn the language of Christmas. Our children know "We

Wish You a Merry Christmas," but they don't know what the Advent means.

The heavenly host that appeared on Christmas Eve might have included all kinds of angelic creatures. When the apostle John went to heaven, he saw four and twenty elders and various beasts and creatures. The books of Ezekiel and Revelation mention different angelic beings. It was a host of celestial beings, including seraphim and cherubim. We commonly believe that they sang, but the Bible does not say that. It says they spoke, boldly articulating, and—from the imperfect tense—declaring continuously, "Glory to God! Glory to God" The angelic host glorified, praised, and lauded Him.

That's why people have lost the meaning of Christmas. That's why your unsaved family members have no respect. The only things they think about are coming over to your house, eating your ham and turkey, making dumb jokes, and getting mad because you didn't give them an expensive gift. The season has become a joke and a fiasco. But the devil is a liar. Praise is going to come out of your mouth this Christmas. You are going to glorify God. You can't afford the luxury of forgetting whose birthday it is. Like the heavenly host, you've got to praise Him.

The heavenly host said, "Glory to God in the highest, and on earth peace, goodwill toward men!" (Luke 2:14 NKJV). *Peace.* The Christmas story brings rest to the weary, wounded, frustrated, and disillusioned. Don't you dare hang your head and seek sympathy from others, looking for someone to take you home for Christmas. If nobody takes you home, you've got company. Who is your company? Peace! Even if you are lonely, you can have a peace that passes all understanding. We celebrate Jesus, His advent, and His coming, for He brings peace on earth.

Goodwill. He brings purpose, fulfillment, and kindness toward men. When you celebrate Jesus and reflect on His coming, you have peace. In the midst of this season, you receive clarity and purpose.

Do you understand what the angels were declaring? A whole host—multitudes—came out of heaven. Can you imagine the sound that penetrated the earth? It must have shaken the ground where the shepherds were, the working men who had never before experienced the supernatural. The men had a supernatural intervention as God revealed Himself to them, and they heard a sound coming from heaven, saying, "Glory to God in the highest! Glory to God in the highest!" We can barely get you to say, "Hallelujah!" for three minutes, but the angels declared continuously, "Glory to God in the highest!"

The Bible says that when the heavenly host departed, the shepherds responded. They got up. Who wouldn't get up in that situation? We'd better get up and go because this Christmas season as God unveils Himself, we must obey. "Let us go and see for ourselves," they said, and when they went, they saw exactly what the angels predicted. They found Mary, Joseph, and the baby, lying in the manger wrapped in swaddling cloths. Then they shared the good news with others.

The problem is, we don't see anything. Too many believers have become blind, dull, lazy, and indifferent, waiting for someone to preach us up and preach us down. We lack the ability to see. When you read Scripture, what do you see? When you get a word from the Lord, what do you hear? The shepherds saw and heard. During this Christmas season, you ought to see and hear something. As you commemorate the coming of Jesus, your eyes should be sharpened and your ears unstopped.

You can't properly praise God and celebrate Christmas because you see and hear nothing divine. You see the television, the mall, and your job more than you see God. The Church has become just like the world. You may as well go out there and join the world because you haven't really seen or heard anything in this great commemoration of the advent of Jesus Christ.

You should have the knowledge of who Jesus is. Your mind should be enlightened about why He came. Your mind should be inspired by the fact that He stepped out of glory. He didn't have to do it. He willingly came and took on the robe of flesh.

The shepherds got a glimpse of the glory and majesty of God wrapped as a young baby, just as the angels said. The baby they saw was not ordinary. He was the Savior of the world. He was the King of kings and the Lord of lords. Like the shepherds, I am privileged to be part of what God is doing. I'm seeing it and hearing it, and I'm getting ready to worship.

The problem is, we don't see it, we don't hear it, and we don't appreciate it. When we come to church on Christmas, our worship is based on what He has done for us and given to us. True worship is about Christ, His disclosure, appearance, and advent, and our nearness and intimacy with Him.

When the shepherds saw Him, their status didn't change. They didn't receive a corporate promotion up the ladder. They were still shepherds, but they had new understanding and supernatural insight. They saw the Christ child, and because they saw Him and were included in the revelation, they owed Him something.

The angels demonstrated the proper response to Jesus. They gave a grand performance. They showed the shepherds how they should respond to Jesus' coming: "Glory to God in the highest!" The shepherds weren't too slow to catch on. The Bible says when the shepherds saw and heard that, they, too, glorified God. The word *glorify* means to "honor, respect, and praise God."

ARE YOU HEARING HIS VOICE?

Christmas is not just a time of fellowship, trying to get along with folks that you dislike, sitting around a table and talking to folks whom you haven't spoken to all year long. It's about who Jesus is. He came to bring peace, joy, and deliverance. The shepherds teach us that when God unveils Himself and includes us in that revelation, it is worth more than silver or gold. When God picks you out, no matter where you are or who you are, you owe Him something. It doesn't matter whether you are on economically high or low ground, whether you are single and raising a family by yourself, or whether your marriage is in trouble. If God decides to choose you, get close to you, and disclose Himself to you, you owe Him worship, praise, adoration, and glory.

Isaiah said, "In the year that King Uzziah died, I saw the Lord" (Isa. 6:1 NKJV). If anything can destroy a nation, it is the sudden death of its leader. We saw it happen in

Israel when President Yitzhak Rabin was assassinated. If anything can mess up a family, it's the sudden removal of the patriarch or matriarch.

Isaiah experienced a sudden, drastic change when his king died. The country was in trouble. Uzziah had been a competent king and a great strategist of war. He brought fame and wealth to the country, but he went too far and God snuffed out his life.

Isaiah had been close to the king, working in the palace. He was slated to be a prophet, but had not yet embraced the prophetic gift because he needed a supernatural experience before he could become a prophet. The Bible says he had to have "the seeing and the hearing."

That's my Christmas message to you. I want you to see and hear something. That is the only way you are going to worship this Christmas—when you see who Jesus is and hear and understand what this season is all about.

During Jewish holidays such as Hanukkah and Yom Kippur, Israelis close their stores, stop work, and devote themselves to the celebration of their holy days. We, too, should be celebrating at Christmas instead of dragging our feet because we can't give our children new coats or have big trees. We have lost the meaning of Christmas.

Isaiah said it's not about that; it's about seeing something. He said, "I saw Him." Who? The Lord Himself. He was "high and lifted up, and the train of His robe filled the temple" (Isa. 6:1 NKJV). Isaiah had been around a long time, but he had never seen Him like that before. That was Isaiah's first time to see God in His splendor, majesty, and glorious position.

Isaiah not only saw something; he heard something. He heard the angels cry, "Holy, holy, holy is the LORD of hosts" (Isa. 6:3 NKJV). The angels declared that the whole earth was full of His glory, but we are dry and empty. We lack relationship with God and divine inspiration and illumination. Unless God gives us money, we can't praise Him. Intimacy and relationship, the unfolding of Himself, are not there. That's why Christmas is empty of true celebration when we should be like the shepherds, crying, "Glory to God in the highest, and on earth peace, goodwill toward men! Joy to the world, the Lord has come!"

If you don't get another job, "Joy to the world."

If your circumstances don't change, "Joy to the world."

We are locked into rituals, but the shepherds had a divine revelation. They saw and heard. If you don't see and hear, then you can't worship and celebrate. You've got to see and hear what God is doing in the land because faith comes by hearing, and hearing by the Word of God (Rom. 10:17). We sit in church, yawning and bored, because we see nothing.

There are times when you can see the shekinah in the house. Everyone else is looking dry, but you see the cloud coming. You can see God's healing virtue coming out of heaven and touching somebody. You can see God reaching down and breaking the back of the enemy. You can see God beating death out of the way. You've got to start seeing and hearing God for who He is—the way, the truth, and the life. He is the El-Shaddai of the universe. He is the King of kings and Lord of lords. He is a wonder; He is amazing; He is awesome; He is mighty; He is glorious; He is altogether lovely.

No one should have to beg you to get up on Sunday morning, dress your children, and bring them to the house of the Lord to celebrate Jesus. Even if you go home to a Christmas tree with nothing under it, that should not depress you if you understand the good tidings. Today, you may be jammed up, but these are good tidings. Tomorrow, God will make a difference. You may be living in hell, but peace can be there, and where the peace of God is, everything has to be quiet. Isn't that what Jesus said to the wind and the waves? "Peace, be still!"

Embrace this season in the advent and commemoration of Jesus Christ. Stop singing dumb Christmas songs that have nothing to do with Scripture. Open up the Bible, and read the Christmas story to your children. Let them read it for themselves. There were not three wise men; there were many. The wise men did not see the baby in the manger; they saw a two-year-old child in a house two years later.

G E T   R E A D Y   T O   W O R S H I P

The shepherds inspected lambs; the shepherds prepared lambs for sacrifice; the shepherds had the awesome privilege of checking Jesus, the spotless Lamb of God who takes away the sin of the world. You are blessed to be included among those who have inspected Jesus Christ. You are blessed to be a part, to be able to give a testimony. Everything that the Bible says about Him is true. I've seen it; I've heard it; I've experienced it.

You've got a reason to celebrate. As you drive your car around doing errands, say, "Glory! Glory! Glory!" Get ready for Christmas dinner, saying, "Glory! Glory! Glory!" And bring your family to your place of worship, saying, "Glory! Glory! Glory!" Celebrate the gift of worship. ❧

A Star, a Stable, and the Savior

🌱 TOMMY BARNETT

As Christmas approaches in Sweden, anticipation mounts for the celebration of the Feast of Santa Lucia, observed every year on the thirteenth of December. To be chosen to participate is one of the dreams of young girls. The winter months in Sweden bring short days and very long, dark nights. Into this blackness the Lucia bride and her court of princesses appear to dispel the darkness with the warm glow of their lit candles, bringing hope and Christmas cheer into the hearts of the people. 🌱 One year a stunning blonde girl from the city of Malmö was selected as a princess. Magnificently adorned in a long white gown, she joined the others, all wearing wreaths of burning candles on their heads. But beneath the candlelight glow was a heartbreaking narra-

tive of loss and loneliness.

Prior to the girl's birth in Helsinki, Finland, a priest delivered a bloodstained note

to her mother. The wish of her dying father, a victim of the war in Russia, was simple:

if the soon-to-be-born child was a girl, he wanted her named Marja.

Although herself ill, Marja's mother also cared for her own alcoholic mother. The

only way to feed the family was by prostituting herself, and the little girl often scav-

enged through garbage cans in search of something to eat. Sick and suffering from mal-

nutrition in those early years, she was sent, along with thousands of other displaced

children, to Sweden. There she moved through a progression of seven orphanages.

Terrified of men and women, destroying dolls and toys, she was a prisoner of her lone-

liness, allowing no one to draw close.

One wonderful day a loving family chose sad-faced Marja, the scared and unloving

little girl who found refuge in the corners of the rooms, to live with them. Her new

father, although a kind man, was an atheist. His wife went to church but did not know

Jesus. Yet an early treasure was a little cross, carefully placed on Marja's bedroom wall, which became a touchstone of faith and courage.

Marja had to cope with another upheaval when her birth mother requested her return to Finland. It was a time of turmoil and terror. She had to endure life with an abusive stepfather. One night when she was in bed with her mother, her stepfather entered the room and attempted to murder both of them with an ax. Although she was barely six years old, Marja pleaded to be allowed to return to Sweden. The caring couple once again took her into their home and soon became her adoptive parents.

The growing-up years were good. She became a fashion model and was honored to be invited to participate in the Miss Sweden Beauty Pageant. Her life was full, but she felt a gnawing emptiness in the deepest recess of her heart—a longing that drew her toward the image of the cross.

At the age of twenty-two, Marja and a friend decided to come to America to meet millionaires or become movie stars. The perception was that everyone in America was rich, so Marja believed it would be a land of plenty and a place that would fill the void in her life. Just before leaving home, she went into her bedroom, paused again by the cross, and in a stirring of faith, asked God to direct her life.

Although the plan was to capture the American Dream, as so often happens, life took a different twist. The only job choices available for the hopeful visitors were as maids or governesses.

After only a week in Palo Alto, California, Marja met a new friend who invited her to church to hear an evangelist by the name of Tommy Barnett. His rapid-fire delivery challenged her English-speaking ability and left her a little confused, but the bedroom prayer in Sweden was about to be answered. She returned to the services the next evening, answered the altar call, and received Jesus into her heart. In bits and pieces, the significance of the Cross was gradually made clear. Three months later, she and the evangelist were married. As her childlike faith grew and became strong, the one who previously struggled to love became the most loving, caring wife any pastor could ever desire.

You see, in being introduced to Jesus Christ, Marja

experienced an everlasting celebration with some parallels to the Santa Lucia event, which honors a historical Italian. During the reign of the Roman Empire, Saint Lucia was born to wealthy Christian parents in Sicily at a time when believers were being severely persecuted and forced to worship in secret. Lucia became engaged to a man of position and wealth who was not a Christian. Her betrothed became angry because she freely and openly gave money to the poor, and he made known to the authorities that she was a Christian. She was soon forced to make a choice: to deny her faith and be married, or suffer the consequences.

THE LEGEND OF SAINT LUCIA

Legend has it that Lucia was sentenced to die by fire, but the fire would not harm her, so she was put to death by sword. After her martyrdom, she became a popular saint because she symbolized the courage and strength of a woman who stood for what she believed.

At Christmas we celebrate not a saint, but a Savior—the One who came into the world in a simple village called Bethlehem. The path from His birth to death was short. He died on a cross to give us not just an annual celebration, but everlasting life. He came to pay a debt He did not owe because we owed a debt we could not pay. His resurrection from the dead is the foundation of Christianity. Everything we believe is founded on that irrevocable act. Jesus' birth is widely celebrated, and while His crucifixion may appear a failure, it is an event that turned into enormous triumph. Only the Christian faith possesses a Savior who took on human form, died for His people, and was raised to a life of power and glory.

In our home and at our church we celebrate Christmas with joy and see the star, the stable, and the Savior as vital symbols and valuable gifts in our Christian lives.

THE STAR STILL GUIDES

Most of us have viewed nativity scenes in many places and depicted in scores of ways. Some are expensive and elaborate; others are very simple. Mary, Joseph, the baby Jesus, a shepherd or two, and perhaps an angel or a couple of animals are gathered around a roughly hewn stable. Often missing, but in my mind mandatory, is the presence of the star: "When they heard the king, they departed; and behold, the star which they had seen in the East went before them, till it came and stood over where the young Child was. When they saw the star, they rejoiced with exceedingly great joy" (Matt. 2:9–10 NKJV).

The star stands out in significance as relevant and vital today as it was when God hung it in space. The Bible tells us that God commissioned a particular star to serve as a travel guide for a group of men from the East who had developed an interest in looking for a child to fulfill a prophecy:

> But you, Bethlehem, in the land of Judah,
> Are not the least among the rulers of Judah;
> For out of you shall come a Ruler
> Who will shepherd My people Israel. (Matt. 2:6 NKJV)

King Herod had different plans for God's newly born Son. Guided by his scribes and chief priests, he was bent on destruction and rejected Christ's divinity. But God's way overturns the plans of earthly rulers.

That brilliantly shining star led to Bethlehem and Joseph, Mary, and Jesus: "When they had come into the house, they saw the young Child with Mary His mother, and fell down and worshiped Him. And when they had opened their treasures, they presented gifts to Him: gold, frankincense, and myrrh" (Matt. 2:11 NKJV).

There must have been an innate sense of awe in those wise men that the star had led them to Jesus. What an accurate travel guide its brightness became to three travelers who set out without a contemporary direction finder, not knowing exactly where they were going. Within their hearts they surely must have known that without the star, they would have been lost.

The Christmas star should be honored because it was put there by the God of the universe. After all, He spoke all the stars into place. It is also a symbol of God's gift of direction to us. It is His travel guide for seekers who will look and follow.

Marja, my dear wife, was a dispossessed waif in a war zone. But from before she was born, God had looked down and placed His arms of protection around her and led her, even as the wise men, toward the cross. The Lord promised, "You will seek Me and find Me, when you search for Me with all your heart" (Jer. 29:13 NKJV). The good news is that even those who may not realize they are seeking Him are still led by some significant sign or event to Jesus.

Many individuals relate miracles of how desperately lost they were in the dark world of sin and devastation when they came to faith in Jesus because another follower of the star shed light on their path. Is it so surprising? Daniel reminds us,

> Those who are wise shall shine
> Like the brightness of the firmament,
> And those who turn many to righteousness
> Like the stars forever and ever. (Dan. 12:3 NKJV)

Travel guides like the Bethlehem star should be honored as we think of Christmas. Faithful parents, friends, and strangers who pray for us, writers of the past and present who teach and lead, are Christmas travel guide stars. It is a challenge to be a faithful, earthbound star, always pointing to Jesus. After all, the greatest asset is the part of us that is the most like Jesus.

Some children who were performing in one of our pageants were asked what they wanted most for Christmas. One little girl from the inner city, who was wearing plain, secondhand clothes but had a radiant face, said, "I want my daddy who is here tonight to meet Jesus. Jesus could make him a good person." She asked nothing for herself, though her need was obvious; she looked beyond herself to her daddy. A contrasting study of economic status was another girl, decked out in the finery wealth provides, who sadly said, "I want Grandma to come to the altar. She doesn't even care about Jesus." These youngsters are proof that "a little child shall lead them." They may be unaware that they are travel guides, like the star, to light the way for their lost loved ones.

The star led the wise men to Jesus. When they found Him, they worshiped and gave Him gifts. Gifts are the heart of Christmas to most people. When I think of what God has done for me and what He has done not just in Phoenix First Assembly of God Church but also at the Los Angeles International Church, I long to give gifts so great that their value cannot be equaled or exceeded—gifts that cannot be purchased.

One year our congregation gave more than $500,000 worth of gifts to needy children and families. More than 130,000 attended the various holiday performances. Their love and generosity were overwhelming and fueled my desire to give gifts that truly only God can give. Those gifts, not equated monetarily, have inestimable, eternal value.

A man who had been bound by drugs and the occult came to Christ in the Los Angeles International Church. He was asked to sing a song he had written for Christmas entitled "He Is the Mender of Broken Hearts."

Members of the congregation in Los Angeles come from broken homes; they are ex–drug addicts, former prostitutes, and people who are displaced and hurting. Their praise, unlike the rather controlled expressions of the Phoenix Assembly, more resembles hoots, howls, and whistles. When the soloist finished, the response was not unexpected. There was not a dry eye in the place, even among the most hardened persons.

As I placed my arm around the man, I told the audience he was blind, but his broken heart had been mended. He returned my embrace, and the man asked what he could give me for Christmas. I had no response. Walking later in the night, reflecting on that young man, I wished above all that I could restore his sight, but that was not mine to give.

What gifts beyond those that can be purchased, wrapped, and placed beneath a tree could be offered, not just to that soloist, but to all those we come in contact with every day? The wise men presented their gifts to Jesus. My desire is to present the gifts that Jesus has offered us all.

The Gift of Courage

One gift would be the gift of courage, the quality of mind and spirit that enables people like the blind singer to face difficulties, dangers, or pain with firmness and strength. Courage is the quality that summons all other virtues of character into action in the face of temptation and crises. In these days we live in, courage is sorely needed.

The biblical leader Joshua needed tremendous courage. As successor to Moses, one of the greatest of the Old Testament heroes of faith, Joshua was fearful. God said,

"Be strong and of good courage, do not fear nor be afraid of them; for the LORD your God, He is the One who goes with you. He will not leave you nor forsake you" (Deut. 31:6 NKJV). Those words of courage were spoken by Moses to a gathering of Israelites. The enemy—more than seven other nations banded together against them—was powerful. The message, "Be strong and of good courage," was battle inspiration for the people. Moses later repeated those words to encourage Joshua, and God Himself repeated the message to him again.

Do the promises in the Old Testament really apply to us, even as that star for direction can guide us on our way? The answer is affirmative. All of these inspired words are to instill courage in us. The apostle Paul, addressing the entire Church, wrote, "So that we may boldly say, The Lord is my helper, and I will not fear what man shall do unto me" (Heb. 13:6 KJV).

When we were pastoring in Davenport, Iowa, my church took a very strong stand against pornography and massage parlors. There were numerous death threats against us and our children. Sometimes a helicopter hovered over our home to harass and frighten us. On many days, a man stationed himself outside our yard and watched our every move through binoculars. It was a time when we needed a God-supply of courage.

One day Marja was driving home from shopping and noticed she was being followed. She knew not to go into our driveway because no one else was home, so she pulled into the neighbor's yard, jumped from the car, and ran into their home through the front door without knocking or ringing the doorbell. The astonished neighbor could hardly speak. She expressed disbelief that Marja could have entered because just moments before she had locked and chained the front door. God supplies what is needed. He will supply, but we must apply.

A deacon tells of being asked to visit a home in his area on Christmas Eve. His arrival was met with a lot of hostility. Caught in the middle of a drunken brawl with decorations scattered among empty bottles, the twelve-year-old boy who had made the call beckoned the deacon into another room. He said he thought people from the church would have more courage to deal with the out-of-control party than the police would. Subsequent visits ultimately restored peace to that home through the

Lord Jesus Christ, and the boy has grown into a strong and courageous Christian.

Likely as not, these days we may find ourselves in the position of Moses and Joshua. The normalization of evil is a plague in our land. It appears that more than seven nations are arrayed against us at times. But low odds are high opportunities with God. We live and move in His promises. His gracious, all-knowing presence is with us, surrounding us, and in us. It calms our fears. Amid our weakness, His courage and strength prevail.

- He provides a way to walk through a locked and chained door.

- He gives power to level the walls of Jericho with the sound of a mere ram's horn.

- He provides the strategy to conquer an enemy like Midian with a few broken pitchers and lamps, or to fell a giant like Goliath with one small stone.

"If God is for us, who can be against us?" (Rom. 8:31 NKJV). Take courage. It is a gift from God designated for you.

THE GIFT OF GRACE

How we need the grace of God in our lives! His unmerited favor is a rich gift from a giving God. Grace is something needed, but not deserved. If we got what we deserved, all would be lost. But God does not give us what we deserve. He gives us what we need—grace.

A drug-addicted, disheveled street mother, dragging little children who were barely surviving their cardboard home, pushed her way into a rescue mission. She was clothed, loved, and told of the grace of the One who was rich but became poor so that we, through His poverty, might inherit the kingdom. A year later she presented her acronym for grace: "God's recipe at Christ's expense."

My son, Matthew, who copastors the Los Angeles International Church, called one of their first Christmas pageants "Miracle on 18th Street." The press picked it up, using the header "What do a camel, an elephant, a gangbanger, and a street person have in common?"

The answer? They were all participants in the Christmas event. Many, with overtones of God's mercy and grace, shared their stories. All of a sudden, a woman in the audience cried out during the performance. An usher took her aside and heard her emotional story. Her son had left home four years previously. Having been forced to move many times, she did not even know if he was dead or alive. As she looked up into the living Christmas tree that evening, there was her son! They were later reunited—all because of God's grace.

My mother used to admonish my sister and me to be sure we asked for what we really needed at Christmas. Many years later, I continue to ask daily for what I really need: grace. It comes in all sizes and shapes—sometimes called mercy, sometimes kindness—but it all comes from above. Grace is a believer's benediction: "The grace of the Lord Jesus Christ, and the love of God, and the communion of the Holy Spirit be with you all" (2 Cor. 13:14 NKJV).

THE GIFT OF PEACE

Our Lord has not only given us the gifts of courage and grace. He has also bequeathed to us peace: "Grace, mercy, and peace will be with you from God the Father and from the Lord Jesus Christ, the Son of the Father, in truth and love" (2 John 3 NKJV).

Such peace was born in the first coming of Jesus. Peace on earth, goodwill toward men. From earliest times, men have sought peace. It has been said that peace seems to be merely the lull between inevitable storms. It is only by knowing Christ and being justified by faith that one has peace with God. The secret is found in God's Word: "Great peace have they which love thy law: and nothing shall offend them" (Ps. 119:165 KJV).

No peace talks and no political agenda will settle conflicts of the human heart in our world situation today with all its struggles, religious conflicts, and political disagreements. Only the Prince of Peace can answer. No wonder the Christmas message resonates:

> For unto us a Child is born,
>
> Unto us a Son is given;
>
> And the government will be upon His shoulder.
>
> And His name will be called
>
> Wonderful, Counselor, Mighty God,
>
> Everlasting Father, Prince of Peace. (Isa. 9:6 NKJV)

THE GIFT OF JOY

One of the greatest gifts available and one that should be put in every stocking hung by a fireplace or in the most beautifully wrapped package under the tree is the gift of joy and humor. The angels proclaimed great joy because of the Savior's birth. Joy should be the flag flung high above everyone who knows and loves Jesus. Jesus said, "In the world you will have tribulation; but be of good cheer, I have overcome the world" (John 16:33 NKJV).

Christians need to appropriate the oil of joy for sadness, the garment of praise for heaviness, beauty for ashes, to glorify God (Isa. 61:3). All are available gifts from the Lord. His is a gospel of joy and fun, the freedom to laugh and to laugh at ourselves. Mark Twain quipped, "If we could straddle the fence and watch ourselves go by in the parade of life, we would laugh ourselves to death!"

I love to laugh and surprise people. Sometimes during a long delay in an airport I'll get a pocketful of quarters, place them in the coin return slots along the bank of phones, and then station myself to watch the priceless expressions of those who find the unexpected dividend. Simple things can be amusing, and people who are genuinely happy are a joy to be around. Here is a question each person should ask himself: Am I fun to live with?

No one enjoys our Christmas events more than I do. When those elephants bow, the white horse walks in, the train comes down the aisle, and the clowns perform their acts, I feel like a child again. My philosophy is that within each of us are a child, a teenager, an adult, and a senior citizen. Taken together, we become a composite of life, all parts of us that have experienced the joy of living.

Solomon was wise with advice that there is a time to laugh as well as weep. If we model Jesus, we see One loved by the children, possibly splashing with them on the shores of Galilee. We read, "God . . . has anointed You [Jesus] with the oil of gladness more than Your companions" (Heb. 1:9 NKJV). We need that same anointing. It is a

gospel of joy and gladness. Let's share that gift, not just on Christmas, but every day of the year. The Lord has come to bring us joy.

I would like to give you the gift of "enough"— God alone

can supply your needs. And the gift of hope—Christ in you is the hope of glory. Take time this season to ask God what His hope is for you, and then respond, determined to fulfill His plan.

There are so many gifts on my pastoral list. God alone possesses them all. Every good and perfect gift comes from above, and He wants to lavishly dispense each one to you: "For of Him and through Him and to Him are all things, to whom be glory forever" (Rom. 11:36 NKJV). He is the Source, Resource, and Goal of every good and perfect thing.

A STABLE

We rarely focus on the lowly stable. Like many in those lands, it was damp, crowded, and permeated with the stench of animals—surely not a place where a child should be born. A thinking person would ask, If God could commandeer a star as a travel guide and give us so many undeserved gifts, why not provide a room at the Bethlehem Inn as grand as any Hilton Hotel for the birth of His Son? At least He could have provided a sterile environment and a nurse for the expectant mother. Is a star a bigger feat for God than a maternity suite for Jesus?

The answer is clear. God could have created whatever He desired, but He made a deliberate choice, which was a stable. His Son was born there because it was part of God's divine plan.

God sent His Son to earth for an important reason. It was a strategic decision not to shelter Jesus from the harsh realities of life. He was not to live the life of the rich and famous. God wanted His Son to experience life in its blue-collar boldness. Jesus' first breath of air burned with odors that surrounded Him. The first sounds He heard were from the animals. His first outfit was made of dust cloths, often called swaddling cloths. From day one, God the Father determined He would not be sheltered from the rough, cruel components of life on planet earth. His purpose was steadfast. Privileged people who are insulated from the rest of humanity cannot relate to the struggles of others. They do not live where most live, eat what most eat, or strive to survive as does most of the rest of the world.

Jesus was born into a real family with few worldly advantages. He worked at a real construction job during portions of His first thirty years. He was part of a neighborhood with friends, and He suffered hardship and misunderstanding. He was maligned and lied about, and He died a cruel death for a crime He did not commit.

Why? Because He was tempted as we are, but without sin. He knew heartache and disappointment; therefore, He understands us. He has been through it. By living in shortage, poverty, discrimination, oppression—a refugee before His first birthday, even betrayed by a friend—He is touched with the feeling of our infirmities.

Look at the stable and be reminded—Jesus understands. He has been where you are and can identify with what you are going through. The importance of the stable is that it symbolizes the foreordained plan of the Father for Jesus to live an unsheltered life. The stable is a monument to His humanness. We, too, must humble ourselves to go to Him, have faith in Him, and pour out our hearts so that we can experience wholeness.

In the stable was a manger, which is nothing more than a feeding trough for cattle. Ordinary in every way, it became extraordinary because the trough became the cradle for a King. The manger symbolizes the transformation of ordinary men and women when Jesus is born into their lives and resides within them. They receive the deposit of Jesus and His Spirit as the resident truth teacher. It becomes an eternal deposit for life. How often I meet people who can say, "Merry Christmas," with the new meaning of a life changed because of Jesus. "Jesus has made my life," they tell me.

Jesus is the center and circumference of every celebration. The significance of the star guides me. The stable reminds me that the very ordinary can be transformed into the extraordinary. Changed people change people. I am but an ordinary man, born to ordinary God-fearing parents who did superordinary things. I am but one who has dared to believe that God takes my nothingness, and when He links it to His almightiness, great exploits occur—all glory and honor to Him. Will you allow that transformation? It is available through the Savior.

T H E   S A V I O R

The angels declared the proclamation, "For unto you is born this day in the city of David a Savior, which is Christ the Lord" (Luke 2:11 KJV).

"For unto you" is as personal as your own signature. There is no denial. It is a universal message, but also an individual one. What will you do with the Savior today? What gift will you give Him? Your heart and life?

"This day" is a very present message. Today is the day of salvation. Today impacts the future. Today is a day to accept or reject His invitation to receive the gift of God, which results in eternal life.

"A Savior"—this is very precious. It is the very heart of the gospel. The road from Christmas to Calvary was very short. This babe of Bethlehem died for our redemption and overcame death for our justification. Without Christ there is no Christmas. Outward merriment all too quickly becomes inward mockery to the starved soul. We celebrate Christmas because Christ came into the world to save sinners!

"For unto you this day a Savior" is personal, present, and precious. Accepting Jesus is the gift of gifts in which He is both the gift and the giver. Augustine wrote, "He loved each one of us as if there were only one of us." It is the message of John 3:16 (KJV) that "God so loved the world, that he gave his only begotten Son, that whosoever believeth in him should not perish, but have everlasting life."

A star, a stable, and the Savior—inexpressible blessings of Christmas. How do we respond to this gift and prepare room for Him in our hearts? Let God arise. Be fruitful this season, and give His best gift to those around you.

There is an Oriental legend of a prosperous elderly man who had a business and sought to choose a successor from three nephews. He handed each a coin and told him to buy something that would fill a room. One purchased a bale of straw, and it covered two sides of the room. Another bought two bags of thistledown, and they filled half the room. The third gave a portion of his money to a hungry man and with what was left bought flint and a simple candle. He lit the candle, and its light filled every corner of the room. The old man blessed the third nephew and gave him the business. His coin was well invested. God's currency is people.

As the Lucia bride and her princesses flood the darkness with their candle-lit crowns, so we, to a far greater degree, must penetrate a lost and dying world with the message of a star, a stable, and the Savior. We are possessors of Jesus, the Light of the World. One candle can light another and lose none of its power. In like manner, we are to take the light of God's love—the ultimate love story from Bethlehem—to the world. Have a blessed Christmas! 🕊

No Gifts
That Christmas

❧ JAMES ROBISON

The greatest act of love in human history was the giving of God's Son as the

sacrifice for our sins: "For there is born to you this day in the city of David a Savior, who

is Christ the Lord" (Luke 2:11 NKJV). What a mighty gift! You see, Jesus was seated at

the right hand of the Father and had all power in the universe. Then He was sent to

earth as a mere man, enduring life in the pit of darkness while setting a great exam-

ple for humanity. In essence, He was royalty beyond measure descending into the

depths of human despair and poverty. The ultimate expression of boundless love was

the sacrificial giving of His life so that we might have life. Jesus said, "I have come that they may have life, and that they may have it more abundantly" (John 10:10 NKJV).

In a materialistic, self-centered society, it is difficult to experience the true meaning of Christmas and receive the potentially life-changing impact of God's matchless gift. Our minds cannot easily comprehend why He, who was rich, would suddenly become poor for our sakes. But Scripture is clear: "You know the grace of our Lord Jesus Christ, that though He was rich, yet for your sakes He became poor, that you through His poverty might become rich" (2 Cor. 8:9 NKJV).

God did all of this because He loved us: "[He] demonstrates His own love toward us, in that while we were still sinners, Christ died for us" (Rom. 5:8 NKJV). Unfortunately, the birth of Jesus and its meaning are often lost in a commercialized setting where Christmas is truly "Xed" out by people's self-centered pursuits.

It is especially sad when Christians dilute or completely leave out the Christmas message. Truly, some Christians seem to worry more about offending a nonbeliever than about sharing their faith. Remember, for those who don't know the Reason for the season, Christmas is merely an observance that doesn't bring true happiness. Aren't we doing our nonbelieving friends and family members a disservice—and missing out on an opportunity—when we avoid telling them about God's wonderful gift of salvation?

S H A T T E R E D   E X P E C T A T I O N S

My journey into the essence of Christmas began when I was a child, and I remember it as though it were yesterday. Although I was only nine years old at the time, the resulting experience transformed my life forever.

I was born in poverty, the result of a forced sexual relationship. An alcoholic forced himself on a practical nurse caring for his elderly father, and I was conceived. The result of that experience was ultimately my birth in the charity ward of St. Joseph Hospital in Houston, Texas.

My mother, Myra Wattinger, placed an ad in a Houston newspaper after my birth asking for someone to care for her little boy. A pastor and his wife, Reverend and Mrs. H. D. Hale, responded to the ad. They took me into their home, and I stayed with them until I was five years old. I called them Mommy and Daddy.

On numerous occasions, my mother visited me and even took me away for short periods of time. It was always a difficult experience, but the Hales explained to me that she was my mother and they were Mommy and Daddy. Although confused, I tried to accept the situation. I spent many lonely days and nights with people I didn't know while my mother ran errands and took care of other matters.

Eventually, the short visits were not enough for my mother. When I was five years old, she took me away from Mommy and Daddy. I can remember hiding under the bed and literally digging my fingernails into the wooden floor as she pulled me, kicking and screaming, from beneath the bed. I did not want to go, but I had no choice.

We departed the greater Houston area and went to Austin. For the next ten years I moved at least fifteen times from one very difficult situation to the next. My mother married a man in his mid-sixties who could neither read nor write. To say we were poor almost seems an understatement.

Among the things I cherished most, however, were the few times that Reverend and Mrs. Hale and Clayton Spriggs—another man who, as a young boy, had come from a broken home and stayed in the Hales' home—visited or sent me gifts. I also had an aunt on my father's side, who was always kind to me and sent me gifts on special occasions. Her name was Roberta Robison, and I called her Aunt Berta.

On each birthday (October 9) and at Christmas, I looked forward to hearing from the Hales, Clayton, and Aunt Berta. They sacrificially invested in toys and clothes, which I badly needed and enjoyed. I appreciated the gifts because I never had the nice things that mean a lot to a child. More significantly, it felt good being remembered by those who loved me.

The year of my ninth birthday we were living in a small, one-room house on the back side of a dump area. The address was 1107 $^{1}/_{2}$ Holly Street. That area cannot be found in east Austin today because it has been totally renovated. The Colorado River, which once ran uncontrollably through the dingy area, has now been made into a beautiful, constant-level lake.

When I was a youngster, living in east Austin was anything but nice. I was a minority—only 10 percent to 15 percent of the people in my neighborhood were white. The rest were Hispanic and African-American. Gangs were prevalent, and I was the frequent target of unkind gestures and beatings. I lived in terror.

But on October 9 I could have cared less about my surroundings. The only things on my mind were the birthday gifts that I expected to arrive. As the minutes and hours ticked by that day, I came to the realization that there was nothing for me— not from Mommy and Daddy, not from Clayton, not from Aunt Berta. I was dismayed and waited anxiously for a few days, a week, and then weeks. Nothing came. Not a word. I thought, *How could the people who love me so much forget my birthday?*

I cannot adequately describe the feelings that tore my heart. I had really believed Mommy and Daddy cared for me and loved me. They always said they wanted to be with me. I truly believed Aunt Berta and Clayton loved me. How could they possibly forget me?

Then it occurred to me: *October 9 is not a particularly memorable day— but everyone remembers Christmas. I bet when Christmas comes, they will make it up to me. Nobody forgets December 25.* I felt a glimmer of hope.

THE CHRISTMAS WITHOUT

As Christmas approached, I water-colored a picture of a tree on a two-foot-by-three-foot piece of paper. I painted some colorful ornaments on the tree and decorated it. The painted picture hung on the wall over a card table. That was our Christmas tree.

Even as I remember it, tears fill my eyes. I saw one or two very small gifts under the tree that I'm certain my mother had sacrificed to provide, but I was waiting for the gifts to come from those who loved me, thought about me often, and could afford to give me something special. All my friends would want to play with my toys, and I would tell them that Mommy and Daddy, my aunt, and my foster brother, Clayton, had sent me the gifts. I was so filled with anticipation, as most children are, that I could not sleep on Christmas Eve. I waited for Christmas to come. I waited for the gifts.

On Christmas Day my mother and I sat in front of that plain piece of paper with the colorful tree. There were no other gifts. They never did come. My heart was crushed. I cried, not just that day and night, but for many days—even weeks—because I felt those who loved me most had forgotten me. As the feelings took root, I convinced myself: *you can't trust people. Those who say they love you cannot be trusted. They don't really mean it. They don't really love you.* My mind played games with me.

The next birthdays and Christmases were the same—no gifts. The situation continued for years, causing me to develop a complex that in many ways damaged my personality as a child and young teenager. Frankly, the effects were devastating enough that they could have destroyed my future. But all of that was about to change.

When I was fourteen years old, my mother suddenly decided I could call Mommy and Daddy and tell them I could visit them for one week. I called, and at the sound of my voice, they began to weep. They said they had missed me deeply.

The next day they came to get me, and I discovered how desperately they wanted to see me and how much they loved me. Still, I was confused about the past few years, beginning with my ninth birthday.

During my stay with them, wonderful things happened. The young people at Memorial Baptist Church, where Reverend Hale pastored, helped me see that Jesus is alive—that He was not only born, but that He died for our sins, rose again, and can live in us.

Mrs. Hale asked the church to pray for me, and one Sunday evening during the invitation, she made her way up the aisle, with tears running down her cheeks, and asked if I wanted to know Jesus. That night I gave my life to the Christ whom God gave to us that first Christmas.

CHANGES COME

While I was visiting the Hales, they assured me that they had not forgotten me. In fact, they had sent me birthday and Christmas gifts throughout the years, but I had never received them because my mother had returned them with a note saying they would not be accepted. She asked them not to send any more gifts or cards. Our telephone number was not provided because for many years we did not have a phone. My mother would not give them our address, and it was difficult to track us because we moved so often.

I did not understand why she cut off our relationship. My first feelings were anger, bitterness, hostility, and even hatred toward my mother. How could she do something so thoughtless and heartless? But then I returned home and during the next months, God's grace began to take effect. Suddenly, the true meaning of Scripture—that He became poor so that we through His poverty might be rich—began to find expression in my heart. No, it was not material wealth or physical riches. It was eternal wealth that cannot be bought with gold and silver. God's grace worked forgiveness and understanding in my heart.

You see, my mother's parents died when she was very young. Her mother passed away when she was nine years old, and her father died when she was eleven. As a young girl, she married a man who said he loved her, but their marriage did not last.

Many men had claimed they loved my mother, but they hurt her and broke her heart. My own father forced himself on her. As a result of being used and abused, my mother lived

a very lonely life full of heartache and pain. Now she had a little son—a son she had to give up for a few years after his birth—but when she took him to live with her from age five through age fifteen, she had a little boy who loved his mother.

And why wouldn't I? When I was taken from the security of Mommy and Daddy, she was all I had, and I clung to her as though she were life itself. I trusted her and had confidence in her, and then when I found out what she had done, I was devastated.

But that indescribable grace working in my heart helped me see why my mother had let me down. She wanted someone to focus his love and attention on her, and when she saw others who had the means to give me nice gifts, she recognized the potential for my heart to be pulled away—for me to be drawn toward those with more ability to provide. She did not want me to become distracted from her or lose my devotion. She wanted somebody—some man—to love her, to hold her. And that man was her own little boy.

I understood, even as a teenager, my mother's great need for somebody to love her for who she was—and I did. Although I was hurt by what she did, God's gift through

His Son enabled me to rise above that pain to live a life full of mercy, grace, and forgiveness for others.

I've been hurt other times in my life, and perhaps some of the pain I have brought on myself. But again and again, God's grace, through His Son, Jesus, has enabled me to forgive and offer mercy to many who have fallen or failed. I have seen God restore people whom most of society and the Church have given up on, and I have watched the miracle of God's grace in action. It's truly a love gift from God: "For by grace you have been saved through faith, and that not of yourselves; it is the gift of God" (Eph. 2:8 NKJV).

When I consider the potential effect of this gift in our lives, my heart rejoices, and I pray, "Dear God, help everyone to experience this Christmas what I did after the Christmas when no gifts came."

THE JOY OF MISSIONS

My wife, Betty, and I can honestly say we've never experienced more joy than through our involvement in feeding programs in hard-hit Africa and other remote areas of the world.

When Peter Pretorious, a committed missionary in South Africa, took Betty and me into Mozambique and showed us the starving children, we were so moved in our hearts that we said, "We must return immediately and begin to secure funds to save these children." We saw how much could be done with so very little, and we knew it was not something from which we could turn away.

We wanted to begin to care for several thousand children immediately, but we had no opportunity to raise the necessary funds through our ministry. We didn't even know if our television viewers and ministry supporters would help with missions. After all, it has been said that if you want to lose your crowd in a church, just call for a prayer meeting or announce a missions conference. Generally, these two events are poorly attended and raise very little interest.

Years ago, our schedule demanded that we travel by air continuously, and for many years we traveled in a ministry-owned jet that could carry the ten or twelve people necessary for our ministry outreaches. I often spoke in two or three cities a day and five or six states in the course of a week. In addition, I conducted more than thirty citywide crusades a year, each of which required preliminary meetings to set them up and gain the necessary support to reach an entire city for Christ.

When God put it in our hearts to save starving children, we were willing to find a way to support this ministry. We immediately sold the airplane and put those funds into saving lives. It was a very difficult move to make because of the demands of our schedule. The plane made us effective in reaching people, and it gave me the privilege of spending meaningful time with my wife and children. Suddenly, the convenience of having a plane was gone. But it is a decision and sacrifice I have never regretted. Betty and I knew we had done the will of God, and the joy we experienced was unspeakable and, as the apostle Paul said, full of glory.

We have seen more than two million children's lives saved as a result of that initial decision. To our delight and amazement, when we shared the opportunity of saving lives on television and with our supporters, a large number of them decided to help.

Some called to say they wanted to personally care for the suffering and dying, so we began to build an effective missions-feeding outreach. Not only have we helped save lives, but we have seen several million people accept Christ as a result of these feeding programs. What an investment! Talk about eternal value and everlasting riches!

Over the years, we have expanded our outreach programs. For example, Franklin Graham called me several years ago concerned about what he had seen in Rwanda. He said, "We went to give medical assistance and found so many orphans that we began to try to take care of them. But we're not prepared for that. James, you need to see what's there."

I sent Peter Pretorious to observe the situation, and he found so many orphaned children that he called me and said, "James, it's the worst thing I've ever seen." I immediately flew to Rwanda. Numerous children, still in trauma because their families had been killed, somehow found their way into my lap.

As I wrapped my arms around them, I discovered that they had also found their way into my heart, so we began to care for those orphans. Thanks to the wonderful response of our friends, we now have the largest orphanage in Rwanda with more than 750 children. We have completed fourteen major buildings at the facility and have about ninety full-time staff members. The Rwandan government told us it's the greatest work in the country and is so effective that they wish they could entrust all of the orphaned children to our care. What a statement!

The Lord has given us other opportunities in Rwanda. Several years ago, I preached in the capital city of Kigali, one of the greatest killing fields in human history. Nearly a million people died there in less than six months. As a result of a five-night crusade in Kigali, we saw more than twenty-five thousand accept Christ despite a 6:30 P.M. curfew, which meant that people had to leave for home before dark.

It is seemingly impossible to reach people in the African culture, but the results of love and a missions outreach, along with the true spirit of giving, have brought about an incredible harvest. In neighboring Zaire (now the Republic of Congo), more than one million people accepted Christ because doors opened to a previously inaccessible country as a result of our efforts in Rwanda. There is no telling what

God will continue to do as those who are led by His Spirit respond in obedience.

The Bible states very clearly: "Love never fails" (1 Cor. 13:8 NKJV). What a shame we too seldom practice it. If ever there is a time of year when our hearts should turn toward God and be in tune with His, it is during the Christmas season. We respond to God's great gift by first giving ourselves to Him and then allowing Him to give Himself to others through our availability and yielded lives.

My sincere prayer is that every reader at this moment will be drawn close to the heart of God, for He is the heart of Christmas. He wants to use you to extend His hands of love to a hurting world.

SHARING THE GIFT

I rejoice when I see my children and grandchildren share God's love. You see, there are needs all around us. You don't have to be Mother Teresa—as great a woman as she was—to show compassion. And you don't have to go to India or Africa to find needs. They are all around you.

Last year, our youngest daughter, Robin, discovered that a little girl in her daughter's preschool class wanted a new doll. She observed that the family probably couldn't afford to purchase a really nice doll like the other girls had.

Because Robin felt deeply concerned for the girl and her entire family, it was in her heart to provide the treasured doll. She asked the mother first because she didn't want to offend her or her daughter.

The mother looked at Robin with tears in her eyes and said, "You have no idea how much what you are sharing means to me and how it will truly impact my little girl. You see, for many months now she has wanted that doll. She is so sensitive to other girls in our neighborhood who have no dolls that she has given some of her own dolls to them. She really believes in her heart that God is going to bless her with a new doll."

Without a doubt, that little girl had come to understand the beauty of giving—something many adults never comprehend—and God rewarded her with a better doll than she had given away so cheerfully.

When Robin offered to buy the little girl the doll of her dreams, the mother knew it would be a true faith-building experience, something her daughter would never forget. She thanked Robin repeatedly for not only blessing the child and the entire family, but also for showing the little girl how God blesses those who bless others.

I pray that all of us will come to see the eternal truth of Jesus' statement: "It is more blessed to give than to receive" (Acts 20:35 NKJV). The Christmas season should remind us of this, and the awareness of God's great gift to us all should inspire us to have the same heart and attitude.

Sometimes our attention is more focused on the box and the wrapping paper than the gift within. One Christmas, a friend of mine gave his son a gift in a very large box. For six months, that child actually played in, slept in, and much of the time lived in that box in the corner of his bedroom.

Children can get so much from so little, yet we waste money, time, and effort trying to give them things that have no effect and often have no meaning. Like children, we too often focus our attention on everything but the gift that our heavenly Father wants so desperately for us to have.

The Essence of Christmas

The first opportunity to see the expression of God's matchless gift in my own life was when I was first able to forgive my mother for her decisions that had such an adverse impact on me as a child and teenager.

God gave me the grace I needed, and my relationship with my mother was very special until the day she went to be with the Lord. I'm thankful to say she was a Christian. She truly loved the Lord very much and, in her own way, sought to serve Him.

Another evidence of God's love and grace working in my heart occurred much later in life when I was reunited with the alcoholic man who had forced himself on my mother. This father I never really knew had hurt me so much, but I was able to forgive him.

I can remember the scene clearly. My father was sick and intoxicated, and as I walked into his small room, I saw that he had thrown up. The stench was awful. Here was a man—filthy and lying in his own vomit—and he was my dad. A man who had never once bought me food, given me any clothes, or provided one area of my care was now lying trapped in a difficult situation due to his own addiction and improper choices.

As I knelt by the very sick man, I pulled him up against my chest and said, "Daddy, I don't know you, but I love you." And I meant it. I prayed with him, I wept over him, and with all my heart I tried to lead him to Christ.

One of my greatest hopes is that when I get to heaven, I will see him. You see, he died a few days after I had shared Christ's love with him. He did not respond, but my hope is that before departing he cried out and said, "God, be merciful to me, a sinner!" And the merciful God, whom we have come to know through the gift of Jesus that first Christmas, gladly received him, and the angels of heaven rejoiced.

I hope when I get to heaven I will see a man step out from the crowd and wave his hand, saying, "Son, look here. Here's your old daddy. I trusted Jesus before I died, and now, through His grace, I live forever."

We must receive this grace, and just as God shared it through His Son, we must share it with others. This Christmas, I invite you to receive God's gift and experience the joy of serving Him. He is more than a baby wrapped in swaddling cloths in a manger, more than a man who lived a perfect life and set a perfect example. I invite you to receive the One who is, in fact, life itself. Our life. Now and forever. *Jesus*: "And she will bring forth a Son, and you shall call His name JESUS, for He will save His people from their sins" (Matt. 1:21 NKJV).

The Secret of Peace and Goodwill

6

JOHN HAGEE

It's Christmastime again, and the Hagees will be having a traditional American Christmas. The tree comes from Canada, the ornaments come from Hong Kong, the lights come from Japan, but the idea comes from Bethlehem. As you know, Christmas is about the birth of a child, so I'll share this little story with you. There was a pastor whose church was in a building program. He was traveling to Pittsburgh to place a special order for the stained glass window that would adorn the baptistry of the new church. When he arrived at the stained glass company, he discovered that he had left the drawing, dimensions, and motto at home, so he wired his wife and asked her to send them to him.

While he was waiting for the return telegram, the pastor happened to tell everyone in the office that his wife was expecting a child. About an hour later a message for the pastor came over the wire. When the clerk read it, she fainted. Her supervisor read it and fainted. The boss read it and turned pale. With trembling hands he gave the message to the pastor, saying, "It's a message from your wife. It says, 'Unto us a child is born, 6' tall and 2' wide!'"

WHAT DOES CHRISTMAS MEAN TO YOU?

Let me ask you a question: What does Christmas mean to you?

A little girl climbed onto Santa's knee in the mall and asked him, "Are you a politician?"

"Why do you ask?" Santa replied.

"Because you always promise more than you deliver," she said.

Christmas in America is supposed to be a time of peace and goodwill toward men.

Sadly, it's not. We are a nation of unspeakable violence—drive-by shootings, drug trafficking, murder, rape, incest, and child abuse—and government corruption. Liberal politicians have mocked authority, demonized men, and deified feminism. They have rejected the traditional family, they have liberated society from its biblical foundations, and then they are amazed that America is falling apart.

Their solutions to these problems? Free drugs, free needles to junkies, free abortions, and free money in the form of welfare checks. These are the proposals of a morally and intellectually bankrupt society.

Peace and goodwill on earth? In the U.S., more than twenty thousand murders occur each year. The Ten Commandments have been thrown out of schools. Prayer is out, and students who were praying in one public school were killed. In America, one woman is assaulted every forty-eight seconds. The evening news in every American city is a visual horror story.

It seems that anyone who calls for America to turn to God is labeled a dangerous, religious zealot who needs to be watched. Anyone who says that criminals should be punished is mean-spirited. Anyone who says the traditional family is the best environment for children is radical, religious, and right-wing.

So, what is the government's solution? It wants to do more research! Who needs $50 million worth of federal research to tell us what we already know? Who needs a research grant to discover that two-parent families are best for children, just as God planned in the book of Genesis and just as He gave to Jesus Christ at His birth in Bethlehem?

A news commentator asked Americans recently, "Has Christianity been tried and found wanting?" The answer is that Christianity hasn't been tried and found wanting—Christianity hasn't been tried by this generation, period!

The Christmas spirit begins with submission and surrender to the Son of God, with obedience to His Word. Until Americans stop treating God like a disease, we can forget about peace and goodwill. They will not happen!

Is Christianity valid for today? The fact is that no

man or woman has ever repented of being a Christian on a deathbed. Never!

Agnostics have repented, atheists have, and backsliders have.

THE SECRET TO PEACE AND GOODWILL

The secret to peace and goodwill is found in the text of Luke 2:13–14 (NKJV): "And suddenly there was with the angel a multitude of the heavenly host praising God and saying: 'Glory to God in the highest, and on earth peace, goodwill toward men!'"

Where are the peace and goodwill that the angels sang about? The angels gave us the secret to peace and goodwill in this message, but we have ignored the conditions that God demands for peace and goodwill. We have ignored the primary conditions and fixed our gaze on secondary results.

We have looked for fruit without planting the tree. We have demanded a rich harvest without planting seed. We have screamed for water without digging a well. We have expected man to be right with man before he was right with God.

Americans are asking, "Where is the peace the angels sang about? Where is the goodwill?" The big question they should be asking is, "Where is the glory to God?" Glory to God comes before peace and goodwill. Glory to God is a primary condition. Peace and goodwill are secondary results. Where is the glory to God? America is expecting a magical harvest of peace and goodwill from people who have no intention of giving glory to God in the highest. Are we willing to do that?

Every Christmas, manger scenes and menorahs are removed from courthouse lawns, and children in school are told they can sing "Frosty the Snow Man" and "Rudolph the Red-Nosed Reindeer," but not songs such as "O Come, All Ye Faithful" with lines offering praise and adoration of Jesus.

Does God get glory in America? Not when it took legal action to allow an eleven-year-old girl in Norman, Oklahoma, the right to read her Bible on the playground. Initially, the fifth grader was told it was a violation of the First Amendment.

Does God get the glory in America? No, not when our government provides explicit sex education beginning in kindergarten. Not when ten-year-old children receive graphic instruction regarding sex and are taught ethics that mock the traditional family. At the same time, prayer, Bible reading, and the name of God cause concern in our courts and educational system. It seems America's public schools are trying to protect our children from the knowledge of God.

Peace and goodwill will never come to America under these conditions. When we give glory to God, then peace is possible—not a minute sooner!

NO UNIVERSAL PEACE

Does this statement shock you: "It was never God's plan for there to be universal peace"? Jesus said, "Do not think that I came to bring peace on earth. I did not come to bring peace but a sword" (Matt. 10:34 NKJV). This means a division between the kingdom of light and the kingdom of darkness. There can be no duality between good and evil. You are either saved or lost. You are walking either the narrow way that leads to God or the broad way that leads to hell.

At a dramatic point in the opera *Faust* the lead tenor falls through a trapdoor into hell. One night the trapdoor malfunctioned, opening only halfway, and the tenor was stuck. A drunken spectator in the balcony stood and shouted, "Thank God! Thank God. Hell's full and I can't go!"

He was very wrong. Jesus said, "He that is not for Me is against Me." James said, "A friend of the world is the enemy of God." In Galatians, we learn that the fruit of the Spirit is love, joy, and peace (Gal. 5:22). I want you to see that peace is a by-product of your relationship with God. Producing fruit takes time, and spiritual fruit comes from relationship. The fruit of the Spirit is peace.

People have tried drugs but found that they do not bring peace. Alcohol does not bring peace. Debauchery will not bring peace. Divorce will not bring peace. Power, pleasure, and profits will not bring peace. Our only chance for peace is submission to Jesus Christ, the Prince of Peace.

Referring to the angelic message in Luke 2:14 (NKJV), "Glory to God in the highest, and on earth peace, goodwill toward men," the latter phrase is misleading. The Greek text reads most accurately, which says, "Peace on earth to those of whom God approves." This is not a declaration of universal peace. It is a fact that peace is impossible without God's approval. Isaiah wrote,

> The wicked are like the troubled sea,
>
> When it cannot rest,
>
> Whose waters cast up mire and dirt.
>
> "There is no peace,"
>
> Says my God, "for the wicked." (57:20–21 NKJV)

Americans want peace but can't have it until they give glory to God in the highest. Peace comes only to those whom God approves, and God approves only the obedient. The idea of a universal peace for a Christ-rejecting, God-hating, pleasure-loving world, enslaved by greed and materialism, is an illusion! Peace is the gift of God, and He gives it only to those who bow before His Son, Jesus Christ, as Savior and Lord.

ONE REASON TO CELEBRATE

There is only one reason to celebrate Christmas, and that is to celebrate the birth of

Jesus Christ. Jesus is the Reason for the season.

The price of peace is absolute surrender. The Bible says,

You are not your own . . . You were bought at a price. (1 Cor. 6:19–20 NKJV)

Every knee should bow . . . [and] every tongue should confess that Jesus Christ is Lord. (Phil. 2:10–11 NKJV)

If you abide in My word, you are My disciples indeed. (John 8:31 NKJV)

Jesus is Lord—you are the servant.

He is the Potter—you are the clay.

He is the Chief Shepherd—you are the sheep.

When you pray, you should say, "Speak, Lord, for Your servant hears," not, "Listen, Lord, for Your servant speaks." Many are willing to serve God, but only in the capacity of an adviser.

Some people may ask, "What about my rights?" You have no rights. You are a servant.

"What about my will?" You must crucify it and be willing to say, "Not my will but Thine be done."

"What about my possessions?" They all belong to God—your house, car, wealth, family, and the Arnold Palmer golf clubs.

"What about my future?" Without Christ, your future will be in eternal hell. Remember, God did not send His Son because He needed us. He sent His Son because we needed Him!

GOD'S CONDITION FOR PEACE

What is God's condition for peace? Absolute surrender! If you want to catch the Christmas spirit, you must first be absolutely surrendered to God's will. People get sentimental over baby Jesus. They sing "Away in a Manger" with misty eyes. They adore baby Jesus, but they reject the risen Lord. Why? Because the risen Lord demands that all men repent and be baptized; confess Him as Lord of all; forsake the ways of the world, the flesh, and the devil; take up their cross and follow Him; and serve Him with all the heart, soul, mind, and body, which is their reasonable service.

Many people do not want to hear this message at Christmas. Instead, they want to hear about a baby in the manger and then walk out of the church and live any way they want and feel good about it. But the baby in the manger has grown up. He is the living, reigning, almighty, all-knowing Son of God. He is the Lamb who has become the Lion of Judah. He is the Baby of Bethlehem's manger who has become the King of kings and the Lord of lords. He is coming again in the clouds of heaven, with power and great glory. He will rule the world with a rod of iron, and He will not ask if people want to obey. He will demand their obedience.

If you want peace and goodwill, God requires you to repent of your sins and become a new creature in Christ; stop lying, cheating, committing adultery or fornication; stop living in idolatry (that is loving anything more than you love Jesus Christ); and stop using God's name in vain (Deut. 5:11).

You also must remember the Sabbath day to keep it holy. People need to get into

God's house and get their lives in order. Some say, "Preacher, Sunday is my only day off!" To which I reply, "Get it right. It's God's day, not your day!"

God demands that you stop hating and start loving; stop being a tale bearer and start being a peacemaker; stop being a greedy, self-serving, lukewarm, compromising Christian and start serving the Lord with all your heart, soul, mind, and body.

PUTTING CHRIST BACK INTO CHRISTMAS

"Putting Christ back into Christmas" has become a meaningless religious phrase in too many circles. If you want to put Christ back into Christmas, you must start obeying the resurrected Son of God. Obedience is the Christmas spirit. It is the secret of peace and goodwill.

How did Jesus get into the manger? I like to picture it this way: the Father placed His arm around the Crown Prince of Glory, and they walked to the outer limits of space and had a heart-to-heart talk.

The Father said, "Men of earth are dying in Satan's dominion. Death, hell, and the grave hold them in slavery. They live in terror and fear. Son, will You go to earth to be born in a stinking cave with the gut-wrenching odor of cattle, donkeys, and sheep? I want You to live in a carpenter's house and know what it's like to run a small business with a tax-and-spend government in charge. I want You to walk through the stench of a scandalous birth.

"Son, Your best friends will betray You. In Your greatest hour of need they will deny You. The organized church will mock You. The government will look for a way to kill You from day one. They will spit on You, slap You, beat You with a whip until You almost bleed to death, and crown You with thorns. Finally, they will take You outside the walls of Jerusalem and nail Your hands and feet to an old rugged cross and murder You between two thieves.

"Son, that's what I want You to do. Will You do it?"

Time stood still. Every demon in hell waited for the answer. Every angel folded his wings in hushed silence. The souls of humanity hung in the balance.

The Son of God looked at His Father and said, "Father, not My will but Yours. I'll do it!"

That's the Christmas spirit—the spirit of absolute obedience. Do you have it?

How did Jesus get into the manger? A Hebrew girl, sixteen to eighteen years of age, was visited by the angel Gabriel. The angel said, "Hail, Mary, thou art highly favored among women. Behold, thou shalt conceive and bring forth a son, and thou shalt call his name Jesus."

Mary's response was, "How shall this be, seeing I know not a man?" (Luke 1:34 KJV).

The angel said, "The Holy Ghost shall come upon thee, and the power of the Highest shall overshadow thee: therefore also that holy thing which shall be born of thee shall be called the Son of God" (Luke 1:35 KJV).

Mary's response could have been, "Not me. I'm not going to be ridiculed by the women of my church. Those long-tongued hussies will crucify me. I can see them counting on their fingers now. No way, Gabriel. Get someone else!"

Or her response could have been, "Never! As a feminist I'm not going to lose my schoolgirl figure over some baby. I have a career. I'm not having anybody's baby!

Marriage is the same as slavery. Being a homemaker is an inferior lifestyle for the thoroughly modern Millie. What do you expect me to do, stay home and bake cookies? Get lost, Gabriel."

A third possible response could have been, "If God does this to me, there is an abortion clinic on the corner. If you think I'm going to live in poverty, have a scandalous pregnancy, ride a donkey to the maternity ward, give birth in a stinking cave, and then let my son be rejected, unwanted, and crucified with criminals, forget it! Abortion is the answer."

But what did Mary say? "Be it unto me according to thy word" (Luke 1:38 KJV). She obeyed with joy, instantly! That's the spirit of Christmas! She said,

My soul doth magnify the Lord,

and my spirit hath rejoiced in God my Savior . . .

For he that is mighty hath done to me great things;

and holy is his name. (1:46–49 KJV)

Please understand this: you obey God only when you do what you don't want to do. If God asks you to do what you want to do, you don't obey, you agree. When He asks you to do what you don't want to do, that's obedience.

GIVE GLORY TO GOD

How do you bring peace and goodwill to your home, your family, your marriage, and your country? God's Word presents God's requirement for peace. You must give glory to God in the highest and learn to obey. God's peace comes to men and women of whom God approves, and His approval comes only to those who obey.

Do you feel you need to give God something in return for His peace? All He asks is that you give yourself. Return to your first love for Christ. Have you lost your first love? Have you ever watched newlyweds? It can be sickening! When they drive down the road, they look like two bodies with one head. They can't seem to walk unassisted, or they walk straight ahead but stare moonstruck into each other's eyes.

If the love of a woman can intoxicate a man to such a degree, it is to our ever

lasting shame that our hearts can be so cool toward Jesus Christ, the Lover of our souls. If He could stand among us today, grieved at the hardness of our hearts, He would say, "You have left your first love." If we loved Jesus passionately, if we loved Him as He deserves to be loved, if we loved Him as He loves us, would not our hearts rise above the casual Christianity that America knows and storm the gates of hell to win loved ones to Christ?

Would our minds be worried about the perfect gift beneath the Christmas tree, or would we grab the horns of the altar and weep for our nation, our families, our children, and our godless society? Would we ask for more and more and more, or would it be more like Mary's saying, "Be it unto me according to thy word"?

When James Calvert went to the Fiji Islands as a missionary to a tribe of vicious cannibals, the captain of the ship said to him, "Mr. Calvert, I feel it's my duty to tell you that if you go ashore among those cannibals to preach the gospel, your life is in great danger."

Calvert replied to him, "I died before I came here. I must obey the Lord."

If you want peace and goodwill this Christmas, give glory to God in the highest, and submit yourself to the will of God in obedience. That is the Christmas spirit and the secret of peace and goodwill. ❧

How to Receive the Spirit of Christmas

7

✣ CREFLO A. DOLLAR JR.

I want to show you how to receive the spirit of Christmas—how to have a "Mary" Christmas — as in the Virgin Mary. I am not trying to exalt Mary above Jesus or claim that she is a deity. Rather, I want to show you how the same supernatural power that was at work in Mary is at work in your life:

> And we also [especially] thank God continually for this, that when you received the message of God [which you heard] from us, you welcomed it not as the word of [mere] men, but as it truly is, the Word of God, which is effectually at work in you who believe—[exercising its superhuman power in those who adhere to and trust in and rely on it]. (1 Thess. 2:13 AMPLIFIED)

The Word of God that you receive exercises superhuman power within you. When you became born-again, you received a word that moved you to come to the altar and give your life to Jesus. The Word was working within you with superhuman power: "For this I labor [unto weariness], striving with all the superhuman energy which He so mightily enkindles and works within me" (Col. 1:29 AMPLIFIED).

When the Word of God is received, it works with superhuman power and energy. It is power beyond anything you can do in the natural.

THE MARY MODEL

Now let's look at the Mary Model and determine why God has given it to us and what we can learn from it. A pattern in the Mary Model can be applied to our lives:

> And in the sixth month the angel Gabriel was sent from God unto a city of Galilee, named Nazareth, to a virgin espoused to a man whose name was Joseph, of the house of David; and the virgin's name was Mary. And the angel came in unto her, and said, Hail, thou that art

highly favored, the Lord is with thee: blessed art thou among women.
(Luke 1:26–28 KJV)

When the Lord is with you, you are blessed and highly favored.

And when she saw him, she was troubled at his saying, and cast in her mind what manner of salutation this should be. (Luke 1:29 KJV)

When the Lord speaks to you, sometimes it is troubling. When I was first born-again and found out that God required me to give 10 percent of my increase, that troubled me. Mary heard a word from the angel, and it troubled her:

And the angel said unto her, Fear not, Mary: for thou hast found favor with God. And, behold, thou shalt conceive in thy womb, and bring forth a son, and shalt call his name JESUS. (Luke 1:30–31 KJV)

The first thing Mary had to do was to get rid of fear. If you walk in fear, you will not be able to follow the Mary Model. The greatest fear Satan tries to put in your life is that the Word of God won't come to pass. He wants you to fear that the Word will not be conceived within you, that you are barren, and that you will never be able to bear fruit.

The angel told Mary that she would conceive and bring forth a son supernaturally. This principle can also be applied to us spiritually. For you, it might be next week's rent, a raise, or a promotion. It might be a family member coming to the Lord. God's Word to you is, "You shall conceive and bring forth!" You can't conceive without bringing forth. Whatever is supernaturally conceived in your heart by the Spirit is going to come forth. If the Word of God is conceived within, it will come forth.

Now ask yourself a question: What have I been trying to bring forth? Perhaps you need peace, healing, or restoration of a broken marriage. The Mary Model shows you how to bring it forth. The Christmas season is a time of spiritual conception—a time when the Word of God enters your spirit, grows within you, and ultimately comes forth through your life.

The angel told Mary, "Call his name JESUS" (Luke 1:31 KJV).

He was named before conception. It is time for you to open your mouth and start calling those things that are not as though they already exist (Rom. 4:17). It's time to call your deliverance forth! It's time to call your healing forth! It's time to call your prosperity forth! It's time to call your favor forth!

Whatever you're believing God for, you must open your mouth and call it forth. God shut Zechariah's mouth because He didn't want Zechariah to speak until he was ready to agree with God. Finally, he wrote, "His name is John" (Luke 1:20, 63 KJV). Then God opened Zechariah's mouth.

Don't say, "I am no good." Don't call yourself a failure. Call yourself what God almighty called you before you were conceived. He called you blessed! He called you healed! He called you prosperous! The angel explained to Mary who Jesus was and what He would do:

> He shall be great, and shall be called the Son of the Highest: and the Lord
> God shall give unto him the throne of his father David: and he shall reign
> over the house of Jacob for ever; and of his kingdom there shall be no end.

Then said Mary unto the angel, How shall this be, seeing I know not a man? (Luke 1:32–34 KJV)

Mary asked, "How shall this be?" How many times have you asked that question? In her case it was, "How shall this be, seeing that I've not been intimate with a man?" In your case it may be, "How shall this be, seeing that my job pays me only $5.15 an hour?" or "How shall this be, seeing that the doctors haven't come up with the cure for this disease?" There is a time factor involved in the anointing:

The angel answered and said unto her, The Holy Ghost shall come upon thee, and the power of the Highest shall overshadow thee: therefore also that holy thing which shall be born of thee shall be called the Son of God. (Luke 1:35 KJV)

The Holy Spirit is your Helper. He won't do what you can do, but He will do what you can't do. The angel told Mary, "For with God nothing shall be impossible" (Luke 1:37 KJV). And Mary said,

Behold the handmaid of the Lord; be it unto me according to thy word.

And the angel departed from her. (Luke 1:38 KJV)

Here are the keys to the Mary Model: "For with God nothing shall be impossible" and "Be it unto me according to thy word."

BIRTHING THE PROMISES OF GOD

Are the promises of God being born in the circumstances of your life? When you read the Word and find something that totally contradicts what the world is saying, are you willing to stand up and say, "Be it unto me according to Thy Word"? When you read the Scriptures, declare, "Be it unto me according to Thy Word!" When you read "by His stripes I am healed," declare, "Be it unto me according to Thy Word!" The Word does not work for some people because they won't release their faith through words.

Take the worst circumstances of your life, and allow the living Word of God to initiate life within you. Get intimate with the Word of God. God's Word didn't remain external in Mary's life; it was internal.

Biologically, in order for a woman to conceive, she must be intimate with a man. During intercourse, hundreds of sperm are released, but only one is needed for conception. Spiritually, it takes only one word from God to be implanted in your spirit for you to conceive.

Getting a lot of the Word is good because the potential for it to work in your life increases. One day you'll be sitting in church and one word will cause spiritual conception. One word from God will impregnate you and change your life forever.

In the natural world, there are many married couples trying to get pregnant, but conception hasn't occurred. As in the natural procreation process, just because the Word is released does not mean you will conceive. You must receive in order for it to enter your spirit and reproduce.

The word *receive* means "to obtain or to get." It doesn't mean to wait until somebody puts it on you. You must receive the Word, so it can work through you with superhuman power and energy.

S P I R I T U A L   A B O R T I O N

Once you conceive, don't let an unbeliever give you a spiritual abortion. When you receive the Word and believe that you have conceived, some unbeliever may come by and say something dumb like, "Your pastor is ripping you off," or "You aren't going to get healed of that cancer. I know somebody who died from the same condition." What is he trying to do? He is trying to cause a spiritual abortion, and you can't let it happen.

Don't let some unbeliever who doesn't know anything about the Bible challenge your belief in the Word of God. The Bible says in Psalm 1:1, "Blessed is the man that walketh not in the counsel of the ungodly" (KJV). Unbelievers aren't supposed to believe it, that's why they are unbelievers. Refuse to let them talk you out of what you believe.

You're not going to talk me out of my faith. It's too late. Why? I've already walked in faith, and I know it works! It's too late for you to talk me out of healing. I've already been healed, and I know it works! It's too late for you to talk me out of sowing seeds. I've already sown, and it works!

PROTECT WHAT YOU HAVE CONCEIVED

I'm not going to let an unbeliever give me a spiritual abortion. I'm not going to abort what I've worked so hard to receive. Now that the Word is living within me, I'm going to protect the seed of the Word. I'm going to nourish it until it is birthed in the physical realm.

Like the seed of a man in the natural womb, the seed of the Word must be in the womb of your heart. When it gets into your heart through your eyes, ears, and mouth, it will bring forth fruit: "A good man out of the good treasure of the heart bringeth forth good things: and an evil man out of the evil treasure bringeth forth evil things" (Matt. 12:35 KJV).

James 1:15 (NKJV) says, "When desire has conceived, it gives birth." In the King James Version, the word *lust* is used. When strong, intense desire is conceived, it brings forth fruit. Now you may have a desire, but has conception taken place? Has the Word of God been conceived in your spirit? It doesn't matter what's going on in your life. The question is, What is going on in your spiritual womb? What is going on in your heart?

The Word of God is compared to seed: "Now the parable is this: The seed is the word of God" (Luke 8:11 NKJV). When the seed of God's Word is scattered, Satan tries to take it out of your womb—out of your heart.

Why is the devil threatening you? He wants you to have a miscarriage. Why does the devil want you to have a miscarriage? Why does he want you to have a spiritual abortion? Miscarriage and spiritual abortion lead to unbelief. You finally get to the point where you don't believe you can conceive or birth things spiritually. Satan wants you to have a miscarriage because he wants you to operate in unbelief.

If you want to conceive spiritually, get to a point of ecstasy with the Holy Spirit—that's when He shows up. You don't look at the clock to see how long you've been in prayer. You just stay!

If the Word of God is not living within you, then you are walking around empty. You are not expecting anything. You aren't believing God for anything. Nothing is going to happen for you because the Word is not at work in you.

FOUR WAYS TO PREVENT ABORTION

When Satan tries to stop your pregnancy, do four things:

1. Worship God

Right in the midst of Satan's trying to abort what has been conceived, lift your hands and say, "Father, I worship You." Sing a song. Put on a worship tape if you can't sing. Make a joyful noise unto the Lord. The highest form of worship is obedience, and when you worship God, you obey Him.

When God told Abraham to take his son and offer him as a sacrifice, Abraham told Isaac, "We are going up the mountain to worship God." In reality, he was going to offer his son. It was an act of obedience. That's the highest form of worship. Do exactly what God tells you to do in spite of what the devil is telling you.

It's amazing how people can hear from the devil better than they hear from God. If you hear from the devil, just take the opposite of what he said to hear from God. If the

devil says you are going to die, start rejoicing because you'll live. Why? He is a liar! He can't tell the truth. Everything he says is a lie. If he says, "Good morning," then stay home. It's going to be a bad day.

2. Magnify God

The word *magnify* means "to make bigger." By magnifying God, you minimize the problem. Mary heard the word of the Lord, and she responded, "My soul magnifies

the Lord, and my spirit has rejoiced in the God of my salvation" (Luke 1:46–47, author's paraphrase).

When the Word of God is living within you, it becomes bigger than your circumstances. When the Word of God inside you becomes bigger than the problems on the outside, you have put your circumstances in proper perspective. We often allow our problems to become bigger than God. We allow our problems to become bigger than the Word.

Learn how to magnify God when you are washing dishes. Learn how to magnify

Him on your way to work. Don't give more attention to the problem and less attention to the Word. Make God bigger than your problem. Make the Word bigger than your problem. Don't sit there and sing the blues—sing praise songs!

3. Keep Your Faith Alive and Let the Devil Know It's Alive

If the devil tries to stop you from doing something, act on the Word. If he is trying to stop you from being a blessing to somebody, then go find somebody to bless. Do the opposite of what he is telling you to do.

4. Become a Distribution Center

If there is one thing the devil hates, it is a distribution center because you become God's hands. You become God's legs. You become God's instrument. There is a spiritual battle over who is going to have the most instruments working on earth. Satan is trying to get instruments through which he can operate, and God is trying to get instruments through which He can operate. Well, I've decided that, as for me and my house, we are going to be instruments for almighty God. We are distribution centers for God. In other words, "Lord, whatever You want done on the planet, I'm Your distribution center. Bring it to me, Lord, and I'll distribute it properly."

If somebody needs love, give me love, and I'll give him love. If somebody needs joy, give me joy, and I'll give him joy. If somebody needs peace, give me peace, and I'll transfer it. If somebody needs money, give me money, and I will share it with him.

It Is Time to Conceive

Christmas is a time for us to look at the Mary Model and follow it step-by-step. It is time for supernatural conception to take place in the body of Christ.

Do you know why people aren't healed? They haven't conceived. People have problems because they haven't conceived. People don't get what they're expecting because they haven't conceived.

Religion says you can do the act without conception, but the Word says if you want results, the Word must enter your spirit, your heart. It's time to stop "playing church"! It's time stop acting religious. It's time to stop having a form of godliness and no power!

I want His power. I want results in everything I do. I want results in my prayer life. I want results in my giving. I want results in my love life. I want results in everything that God says I'm supposed to have!

John declared, "Greater is he that is in you, than he that is in the world" (1 John 4:4 KJV). What's inside? It's the anointing. But if conception of that Word has not taken place in your heart, then you have no anointing in you.

Mary said, "I have received. Be it unto me according to thy word." Be it unto me according to everything that God has said in His Word. I'm not going to argue with it, try to figure it out, or wonder how it will work. Be it unto me according to His Word! I receive it, God! I open myself up! Be it unto me according to Thy Word!

When the Word gets in you, it is superhuman power and energy working on the inside to create what the world cannot believe:

❧ They couldn't believe Jesus could be born to a virgin, but it happened.
(Luke 1:30–35; 2:4–7).

❧ They couldn't believe Jesus would be raised from the dead, but it happened
(Matt. 28:2–7).

❧ They couldn't believe a man could go down in water seven times and come up
healed of leprosy, but it happened (2 Kings 5:9–14).

❧ They couldn't believe clay on a man's eyes could give him his sight, but it
happened (John 9:1–7).

❧ They didn't believe Jesus could feed more than five thousand people with a
few loaves and fish, but it happened (Mark 6:35–44).

❧ They didn't believe a widow could have her dead son back, but it
happened (Luke 7:11–17).

And the same Jesus who caused all these things to happen can cause your household to
get right, save your mate, heal your body, and solve your problems.

It is time for God's people to conceive spiritually. It is time for the seed of God's Word to enter your heart. It is time for you to make up your mind to willingly receive the Word. Don't debate it. Don't doubt it. Determine that the Word going into your heart will cause superhuman power and energy to work on the inside.

You may be trying to figure out how everything is going to turn out. You may not see how your situations will work out, but something is at work inside you that is far greater than the circumstances on the outside. There is something growing within you.

When a woman is expecting a child, her body changes. It adapts and makes the necessary adjustments to carry the baby. If more room is needed, her body has the ability to expand to make more room. If you want to have the Word of God living within you, you must become adaptable. It may not be easy where you are right now, but adapt. Make up your mind to adapt.

Someone may say, "You don't understand. They turned off my power." Get a candle! Light the candle! Why? I'm adapting because morning is coming soon.

Maybe you don't have nice things right now. Perhaps your husband left you or your job is not paying you sufficiently. Adapt. Instead of going out and buying steak

and lobster, buy beans and franks. Why? Because the Word of God is at work within

you, and you know it is not always going to be like this. Something is coming forth!

Something is about to be born! So adapt!

People around you are looking at you. They don't understand why you act the way

you do. You are lifting your hands and praising God when you ought to be crying.

They think you should be insane by now. They can't figure it out. They don't know

that the Word of God entered your heart one day, and once the Word has entered, the

manifestation shall come forth.

Keep praising God because when you get to a certain point in praise, you will no

longer have to try to get things to happen; they will happen. When Mary became preg-

nant, she began to magnify the Lord. She began to praise

God. She wasn't wondering if she was going to conceive. She

was already expecting, and her soul magnified the Lord.

Once the Word of God is living within you, you won't

have to try to convince people that it is there. The Word in you will be evident. The Word will eventually come forth. However, don't expect things to come forth without being willing to push. When the time comes, push to bring it forth.

God majors in taking messes and making them masterpieces. He majors in taking you from mediocre to magnificent. All you have to do is give Him the opportunity by letting the Word work within you with supernatural power and energy, and you will receive the true spirit of Christmas. Have a "Mary" Christmas! ॐ

About the Authors

Tommy Barnett pastors the Phoenix First Assembly of God, one of the largest Assembly of God churches in the United States. He also founded and copastors the Los Angeles International Church, has authored numerous books, and hosts a weekly television program. John Bevere is the founder of John Bevere Ministries in Orlando, Florida. He is also a popular speaker and the best-selling author of several books, including *The Fear of the Lord* and *The Bait of Satan*. Dr. Creflo A. Dollar Jr. is the founder and pastor of the 20,000-member World Changers Church International in College Park, Georgia, and a world-renowned author and international conference speaker. John Hagee is the founder and pastor of the 17,000-member Cornerstone Church in San Antonio, Texas, and the author of best-sellers such as *Final Dawn over Jerusalem*, *Beginning of the End*, and *Day of Deception*. Jackie McCullough has spoken internationally, serves as associate pastor at the Elim International Fellowship in Brooklyn, New York, and is president and CEO of Daughters of Rizpah. James Robison is the founder of LIFE Outreach International and reaches more than 60 million homes throughout the U.S. and Canada with his television program, *Life Today*. Ron M. Phillips is a leader in broadcasting and pastors Central Baptist Church of Hixson, Tennessee.

Also from
Thomas Nelson Publishers
for the Holiday Season

The Heart of Christmas

Six great Christian communicators help you find delight in the symbolism of the nativity scene, discover meaning behind Jesus' name, journey with the wise ones who follow God to unexpected places, and get to know Mary and Joseph a little better. Contributions from Max Lucado, John C. Maxwell, Jack Hayford, Bill Hybels, David Jeremiah, and Rick Warren will remind you of the wonder, beauty, and truth of this season of celebration.